The

Christopher Bollas

Routledge
Taylor & Francis Group

LONDON AND NEW YORK

First published 2009 by Routledge
27 Church Road, Hove, East Sussex BN3 2FA

Simultaneously published in the USA and Canada
by Routledge
270 Madison Avenue, New York, NY 10016

Routledge is an imprint of the Taylor & Francis Group, an Informa business

Typeset in New Century Schoolbook by Garfield Morgan,
Swansea, West Glamorgan
Printed and bound in Great Britain by TJ International Ltd
Padstow, Cornwall
Paperback cover design by Andy Ward

This publication has been produced with paper manufactured to strict
environmental standards and with pulp derived from sustainable forests.

British Library Cataloguing in Publication Data
A catalogue record for this book is available from the British Library

Library of Congress Cataloging-in-Publication Data
Bollas, Christopher.
  The infinite question / Christopher Bollas.
      p. cm.
  Includes bibliographical references and index.
  ISBN 978-0-415-47391-0 (hardback) – ISBN 978-0-415-47392-7 (pbk.)
1. Association of ideas. 2. Free association (Psychology) 3. Subconsciousness.
4. Psychoanalysis–Case studies. 5. Dream interpretation. 6. Freud, Sigmund,
1856–1939. I. Title.
  BF365.B65 2009
  150.19'5–dc22

                                                                2008023476

ISBN: 978-0-415-47391-0 (hbk)
ISBN: 978-0-415-47392-7 (pbk)

The philosophical axiom: Thought must be
understandable on the basis of being.
The psychoanalytic axiom: There is unconscious thought.

Alain Badiou

Contents

Introduction

This book explores how people express themselves unconsciously through free association in a psychoanalysis.

We do not need to be psychoanalysts to know that as we go about the business of an ordinary day we perceive events around us unconsciously. In doing so, we also think unconsciously about these events and link them to prior experiences in our lives, and some of them may be organised into a dream that night.

A small portion of what we think about unconsciously will have dipped in and out of consciousness. Driving past a dairy farm, I might think of my early childhood when I lived in the country. I might remember my weekly trip to the dairy with my grandfather, and the experience of clutching shoots of tall grass and pushing them through the fence so that the cows – massive, snorting beasts – would open up mouths with sandpaper tongues to grasp the offering. I might think of that consciously, but I might not. If I were to go down memory lane I could add dozens more impressions of my visits to the dairy. I could write about my grandfather's Model T Ford, in which he put me on his lap and let me turn the steering wheel; where we stopped for ice cream; when we visited the feed store, where I could climb the small mountains of grain.

But let's imagine that I do not think of any of these memories as I drive by a modern dairy. They do not enter consciousness. I might turn to my wife and children, however, and ask, 'Would you like to stop for an ice cream?' Would I be aware of the link between driving by the dairy and the trips with my grandfather? Ordinarily, no. But obviously it is in my mind – we can see it through the associations that follow the sight of the 'evocative object',[1] the dairy. It is, therefore, something I am thinking about unconsciously. And the 'me' that thinks that way is a much more complicated 'me' than the 'me' that thinks consciously. When I think consciously I can think only one thought in any given moment. Yet an image, such as my grandfather standing with me by the dairy fence, simultaneously contains many thoughts. The image, worth a thousand words, is an unconscious organisation.

A day in our lives is a complex journey through a maze of associations. We cannot possibly think all the impressions that stimulate us. We cannot even think all the associations sprung by a single evocative object. A dairy farm for me, as we see, has hundreds of memories embedded in it. (Freud wrote that the unconscious contained 'clusters of associations'.) Add to that single image something which I have elsewhere termed the 'lexicon of objects',[2] and we are surrounded by *thousands* of evocative objects embedded in reality. These objects serve as the terms of our thinking.

Each of us is a hidden novelist, composer, painter, sculptor, dancer. We compose – through language, sound, image, gesture and movement – thousands of unconscious ideas about the world in which we live.

Readers of Freud's *The Interpretation of Dreams* will find there two quite different theories of the unconscious.[3] The first six chapters of his work explore the many different types of dream and the various ways in which dreams are constructed. Freud repeatedly – although usually through the work of other authors, whom he quotes extensively – acknowledges those dreams that weave lived experience into the text of the dream. In Chapter 1, Section C, 'The Stimuli and Sources of Dreams', Freud cites many writers who illustrate how the dreamer incorporates a stimulus into a dream. (For example, Freud quotes extensively from Paul Wilhelm Jessen, who wrote: 'A peal of thunder will set us in the midst of a battle.'[4]) In Freud's essay on the unconscious, written some fifteen years after the dream book, he adds that the majority of unconscious ideas are non-repressed contents.[5]

Why is this distinction important?

Psychoanalysts have virtually ignored the so-called non-repressed unconscious in favour of the repressed unconscious. Nowadays the repressed is regarded as being the essential core of Freud's theory of the unconscious; in fact, it has become synonymous with the idea of Freudian conflict – the mind pitted against itself.

Freud's theory of repression, as a clinical reality, focuses on the return of the repressed. Repressed ideas return via 'derivatives' that can bypass the censorious part of the mind which disapproves of the unwanted ideas. Analysts listening for these derivatives will find them, for example, in slips of the tongue, or in single words that carry within their phonemic structure other signifiers that sneak the unwanted past the censor through a grammatical sleight of hand. This form of practice may demand that the analyst remain largely silent for weeks on end, as both analyst and analysand await the arrival of such derivatives.

However, Freud also consistently proposed another theory of unconscious expression, one that does not centre on the more rarefied and arcane moments when a derivative suddenly appears out of the plethora of associations. This other theory suggests something more radical: that implicit in the sequence of our thinking there is a serial logic; that if we listen to the leaps in the speaker's associations, from one topic to another, and then to another, that a line of unconscious thought – or, more accurately, many lines of thought – will be found in the sequence.

Although I consider it a valuable theory of one form of unconscious thinking, this book will not focus on Freud's theory of repression. I shall, instead, concentrate on his theory of sequence, not only because it has been largely ignored within the psychoanalytical community but, more importantly, because I believe that if we learn to listen to that sequence, we will discover a richer and more complex unconscious speech than is to be found in the occasional lone signifier bearing some specific phonemic promise.

What is 'the logic of sequence'?

Even when we have a conscious agenda, such as writing a list of things to buy at the grocery store, our thinking does not usually follow a simple, predetermined path. We may have a few things in mind as we start to write, and we may start to list them – but then we will get stuck and have to wait until objects still in our unconscious mind pop up into consciousness. And on our way back from the grocery store we may be struck, suddenly, by the things we forgot to put on the list. So even a deliberate attempt to order our thinking consciously is unlikely to meet with complete success.

When we are not bound by an immediate agenda, our thoughts move in an undirected sequence that would appear to be random. However, Freud discovered that if we speak these thoughts as they pass through our mind, they reveal an inherent 'logic of sequence'. Beneath the manifest thoughts, the apparently disparate ideas illuminate another, deeper text: there is a hidden logic of which we are unaware until we grasp, in retrospect, the pattern that is implicit in the line of seemingly unconnected ideas.

Is this not, then, the ghost in the machine through the back door? If we say that the manifest ideas reveal a hidden logic, something between the lines, is this not proposing some other thinker – other than ourselves? And who would that thinker be? This is only the way it seems. In fact, we are engaged in unconscious thinking all the time, even when we are asleep. Conscious thinking and unconscious thinking are different *forms* of thought, both carried out by the same person. While I am reading a novel I might elect to listen at the same time to a Schubert quintet. Although the two activities – reading the printed word, listening to composed sound – are different, we do not need to posit that I am two different people as I attend to each of these different *forms* of thought. In the same way, we do not need to suggest that we are two different beings when we are thinking unconsciously and consciously.

What we think about unconsciously, how we think it, where it leads us, how it involves us in different interests: these aspects of unconscious thought create traces in the sands of consciousness. We can thus observe some of the patterns of unconscious thought, but observing its effects and identifying *why* we think this way are very different matters indeed. These and scores of other questions we cannot answer for the simple reason that we do not have access to this part of our mind. We know it exists, we know that we think unconsciously, and our actions (interests, attractions, distractions, avoidances, and so on) indicate this – but we shall not know the ultimate logic of that indication.

However, when we hear from Arlene, Caroline and Annie – the three women of this text – we shall discover that the logic of free association is unconscious thinking on the verge of becoming conscious. In Chapters 10 and 11 we shall return to the challenging discovery that analysands select specific issues to focus on *before* thinking about them consciously.

This book inherits a problem that Freud encountered when addressing unconscious thinking and articulation. In *The Ego and the Id* he described how the unconscious refers both to repressed mental contents and to the agency that performs the act of repression.[6] It refers to contents but also to process. So when discussing '*the* unconscious', how do we determine whether we are referring to unconscious processes or to the mental contents (memories, desires, character features, and so on) of the self?

In part, the problem is simply grammatical. I could leave out the article, and specify each time 'unconscious processes' or 'unconscious contents'. That would at least meet contemporary objections to the idea of there being something we could term *the* unconscious, as if it were an inhabiting thing inside us. However, as I do not want to imply that this problem can be simply resolved by losing the article, I shall assume that the *context* in which the signifier 'unconscious' is used will indicate whether I am referring to those ideas within a person's unconscious or to those processes of thought that arrange the ideas.

Freud's distinction between the unconscious and the preconscious has raised as many problems as it has solved. In so far as the preconscious refers to *contents* in the mind, it describes that which is resident in the descriptive unconscious, but is available to the conscious mind. It differs, therefore, both from material that has never entered consciousness, and from ideas that have been censored and repressed. A confusion arises, however, over the fact that preconscious ideas are not simply stored in one's unconscious somewhere; the agent of their disposition is also unconscious. The preconscious must operate according to unconscious processes, unless the theoretician seeks to reach the absurd position of arguing that we are consciously manipulating preconscious contents!

I have written elsewhere about 'the receptive unconscious' and 'the received', juxtaposed with the repressed unconscious and the repressed. I find this a useful distinction – but I would be guilty of making the same error I have just addressed if I did not make it clear that the repressed, the received and the preconscious are simply different forms of unconscious thinking. This issue will be discussed at greater length in the final chapter.

The question of whether one is referring to form or content is addressed, in part, by the introduction of an image. If we imagine it as a symphonic score, we can visualise both the contents and the processes that are signified by the word 'unconscious'. Indeed, in the beginning of the self, unconscious process and unconscious contents are one. Our unconscious life originates *in utero*, derived from our inherited disposition, and it continues to develop through the formative years of childhood. The ways in which we are handled by our early others – the transformational objects of our infancy and childhood – are codified within us and become part of the grammar of our ego, or the rules for being and relating that we employ in the ways we live our lives. In this respect, process (or form) is indistinguishable from content. The same is true for any work of creativity. The way Brahms composes (forms) his musical ideas (contents) melds both process and content into one organic entity.

Indeed, we can isolate any content (in analysis, in fiction, in musical composition) and study that particular 'piece'. But the person free associating in analysis (and the work of fiction, and the musical composition) are all 'moving' experiences. If we isolate one moment we do so by removing that fragment from the process of the work. In the same way, when we isolate an unconscious idea by removing it from its processional context and function, we temporarily ignore the unconscious as a process of thought.

This work is not a philosophical disquisition, nor is it an attempt at an exhaustive study of unconscious forms of thought. It is intended simply to restore interest in the Freudian method, particularly in free association. By providing clinical vignettes I hope to illustrate how we can follow the analysand's free-associative logic.

The main focus will be on the narrative line of thought in free association – because Freud was specifically interested in discovering the logic of sequence that revealed unconscious lines of thought. However, I would not want to pursue this strictly 'classical' way of thinking about a session without at least indicating the presence in the hour of many other forms of thinking and expression. As you will see, I propose that we term these different forms 'categories' and 'orders' for purposes of clarity.

Although this book addresses some of the theoretical aspects of free association, the core of the text resides in the three cases presented in Chapters 7–9. The book is intended to provide both newcomers and seasoned analysts with material to chew on and cogitate over at their own pace.

Readers of this book may find it useful to study its companion volume, *The Evocative Object World* – especially the first chapter, on free association – as it may serve as a useful introduction to the issues raised in this work.

Acknowledgements

I want to thank the members of the European Study Group on Unconscious Thought (ESGUT) for their help over the last twenty years in studying the many forms of unconscious expression. Analysts from England, Sweden, Switzerland, Germany and Italy have spent hundreds of hours poring over clinical material with a simple question: what do we learn from many readings of a single session? The answers we have discovered have taken us along many paths, repeatedly renewing our relation to the primacy of the task. What do our patients teach us? Although we have learned a considerable amount from this collaboration, we are all united in one conviction: psychoanalysis is in its early – very early – stages, and there is more to be learned from it than we ever imagined.

I am grateful, in particular, to my colleagues in Great Britain and their patients for permission to publish sessions from their analyses.

I also want to thank Sarah Nettleton and Robert Timms for their editorial help and astute guidance.

Alain Badiou (1992) *Infinite Thought*. London and New York: Continuum.

1

This world without end

In *The Interpretation of Dreams* Freud proposed that a dream organises mental issues of 'psychic intensity' that occur during the day into highly condensed images (the dream) that weave such daily experiences into the psychic history of a self. 'There is no need to underestimate the importance of the psychical intensities which are introduced into the state of sleep by these residues of daytime life,' he wrote,[7] curiously anticipating his own subsequent neglect of this form of unconscious organisation.

Discussing the mechanisms of dream formation, Freud explained: 'The first thing that becomes clear to anyone who compares the dream-content with the dream thoughts is that a work of *condensation* on a large scale has been carried out.'[8] He argued that a dream is organised during the day – indeed, it may take several days to appear – and the demands of the various ideas competing for representation mean that they have to be converted into images that can embody many ideas at one time.

Later in the dream book Freud argued that the manifest dream content reflected the work of a censor – in other words, that the images were distorted in order to avoid transparency. This could indeed be one reason why the unconscious would employ the mechanism of condensation. In opting for a theory of dream life organised centrally around evasion of the censor, Freud seemed to limit his theory of unconscious thought. He was, however, quite aware that there was more to it than this. In his essay on the unconscious he wrote: 'everything that is repressed must remain unconscious; but let us state at the very outset that the repressed does not cover everything that is unconscious' – indeed, 'the unconscious has a wider compass: the repressed is a part of the unconscious.'[9]

In distinguishing between the repressed and the descriptive unconscious, psychoanalysis developed an unnecessary privileging of so-called dynamic, repressed unconscious material over other ideas that happened to be in the unconscious but were not conflictual and were not part of the sexual or aggressive dynamic. However, in order to appreciate fully the richness of Freud's dream book – especially his crucial theory of condensation – it is necessary to recognise that he proposed, by implication, a comprehensive theory of unconscious thinking that involved far more than the simple concept of repression.

Indeed, readers of the dream book must at times wonder why, if the forces of repression were so powerful, Freud was able to decode a dream with such success. Psychoanalysts working with a patient's dreams, at least in my experience, do not tend to encounter some powerful censor seeking to divert elucidation of the dream. On the contrary. As one works with a dream, breaking down its single images into thousands of words, the analyst discovers, generally without too much resistance, a remarkable universe of thought. Indeed, long before Freud, we observe a conscious interest of people in what their dreams 'mean'.

In fact the availability of dreams for associative deconstruction poses quite different problems. The censor here is time itself. A dream opens a door to an infinity of meaning, yet few psychoanalysts and analysands these days are able to devote the time that Freud gave himself in the dream book to the exploration of a single dream.

By opting for the dynamic unconscious – the unconscious that carries conflicted sexual and aggressive dimensions – as the privileged order to which the analyst should attend, Freud finds a concept that assumes the function of a fetish. This theory will now ward off the unknowable depths that face all analysts – as they can now focus on seeking selective facts of a sexual or aggressive type. It is

as if focusing on primal scene only

ironic indeed that these two drives would assume this fetishistic function, but it should not be altogether surprising, given Freud's concept of a compromise formation.

What was the compromise? Freud essentially paid off the part of him which knew very well that unconscious mental life was deeply complex and far too intellectually attenuated to be guided entirely by sexual or aggressive drives and contents – but he had to offer up something that seemed credible as a stand-in for facing the unknown. Late-nineteenth-century Vienna could accept that dreams were encrypted visions of sex and violence; but it was too challenging to allow that they might be unconscious forms that thought the entirety of psychic life. Freud elected a kind of *Reader's Digest* version of mental life – full of the romance of the sexual and the aggressive – to divert attention from the fuller implications of the world he discovered.

And what was that world?

In discovering the dream thoughts – revealed through free association – Freud wrote that they 'emerge as a complex of thoughts and memories of the most intricate possible structure, with all the attributes of trains of thought familiar to us in waking life'. As an afterthought he added that 'they are not infrequently trains of thought starting out from more than one centre, though having points of contact.'[10] Just over two hundred pages later in his dream book, Freud returned to this insight: 'It is, indeed, not easy to form any conception of the abundance of the unconscious trains of thought, all striving to find expression, which are active in our minds.'[11] No indeed, it was not easy. Freud consistently asserted that all these complex ideas had instinctual origins, but such a view reflected an almost auto-erotic evasion of his remarkable discovery – that the human mind moved according to a vast Mahlerian symphony of lines of thought emerging from different sources, converging now and then, and then radiating out to infinite space.

'The dream-thoughts to which we are led by interpretation cannot, from the nature of things, have any definite endings,' he wrote in the dream book. Approaching this unbounded world – not sealed in the order of the drives

– he pushed on: 'They are bound to branch out in every direction into the intricate network of our world of thought.' What, then, could we possibly discover from this world without end? 'It is at some point where this meshwork is particularly close up that the dream-wish grows up, like a mushroom out of its mycelium.'[12]

I think Freud puzzled about why certain unconscious ideas are discoverable and others radiate out into infinity, never to be discovered. The challenge this poses – the infinite, the finite – certainly permeates our task in this book as we examine sessions from Arlene, Caroline and Annie. I think we will appreciate the dilemma facing Freud. 'The most complicated achievements of thought are possible without the assistance of consciousness,' he wrote, implicitly recognising, in my view, that he knew he could never tell the story of the unconscious.[13] Twenty pages later he added a coda:

> The unconscious is the true psychical reality; in its innermost nature it is as much unknown to us as the reality of the external world, and it is as incompletely presented by the data of consciousness as is the external world by the communication of our sense organs.[14]

Freud (and subsequent psychoanalysts) defended against the complexity of this descriptive unconscious through the fetishisation of sexuality and aggression. It is ironic, therefore, that it was Freud himself who found a way to listen to the logic posed by the infinitely complex world of unconscious articulations.

2

A specially intrinsic connection

Freud acknowledged in *The Interpretation of Dreams* that there were many kinds of dreams, including those whose meaning was transparent: 'While some dreams completely disregard the logical sequence of their material, others attempt to give as full an indication of it as possible.'[15] However, it was the more complex, perplexing dreams that most drew his psychological attention. He argued that although such dreams defied easy understanding, this did not mean that they were without their own logic; indeed, they bore within their momentum an intrinsic connective reasoning.

Such dreams, he wrote, 'reproduce *logical connection* by *simultaneity in time*'.[16] He then associated to Raphael's frescoes in the Vatican and *The School of Athens*, in which various poets and philosophers are represented pictorially in one group, brought together by association. 'It is true that they were never in fact assembled in a single hall or on a single mountain-top,' he wrote, 'but they certainly form a group in the conceptual sense.'[17]

It is at this point in his thinking that Freud concludes that dreams have a certain temporal logic. Acknowledging that dreams present details with precision, he notes:

Whenever they show us two elements close together, this guarantees that there is some specially intrinsic connection between what corresponds to them among the dream-thoughts. In the same way, in our system of writing, '*ab*' means that the two letters are to be pronounced in the single syllable.[18]

Moments later he declared that there were two observable causalities in thought. 'In both cases *causation* is represented by *temporal sequence*: in one instance by a sequence of dreams and in the other by the direct transformation of one image into another.'[19]

Here, pulling back perhaps from impossible questions – What does a dream mean? What does it represent? – Freud rests on the rocks of phenomenology to catch his breath. He notices, almost in passing, that a dream's logic resides in part in its sequence of ideas.

From his observation that dreams flow according to a sequential logic, Freud would then discover his laws of free association. So far as the speaker was concerned, this was designed to be a discourse free of conscious linear sense – the subject was to enjoy a certain liberation from the knowledge of logical thought. Crucially, however, Freud realised that the *order* in which a person said what was on his or her mind revealed its own intrinsic logic.

This leap in Freud's theory of the unconscious, however, was – and is – relatively unexplored. His theory of repression rested on the dramatic 'accidental' moment – the slip that was to become linked to his name, when a person would spill the beans and have to grin and bear it. However, he never abandoned this other theory of unconscious communication. True to his observing mind, he had noticed a less juicy and more mundane aspect of speech: the temporal logic of unconscious articulation. All the time the patient was talking, he or she would be exposing through the simple order of spoken thoughts a hidden logic that was ultimately more revealing than the embarrassing moment heralded by the slip.

As we shall see in the cases to follow, it is this serial logic that discloses the subject's desire, anxiety, memory and conflict. Embedded in the clusters of association – the assemblage of many lines of thought – Freud found the voice of the unconscious. Unlike the slip of the tongue or the relation between signifiers, this unconscious thinking functions not only in the verbal context, but also in the worlds of musical thought, painting thought, movement thought – indeed in all expressive arts, as each articulates – its own contents through a sequence within its form.'

3

Weaving in the factory
of thought

In asking a dreamer to free associate, Freud was not soliciting the dreamer's ideas *about* his or her dream. He was not turning to consciousness, either his own or the analysand's, to see how they could figure it out. Instead, he took the view that the dreamer should simply report what he or she was thinking in the moment, regardless of how insignificant it seemed. In the days of the dream book Freud asked patients to shut their eyes when talking: 'I began the treatment by assuring him that if he shut his eyes he would see pictures or have ideas, which he was then to communicate to me.'[20]

The strategy was clear.

Freud asked his analysands to situate themselves in a dream-like place because he found that ideas spoken in this free manner (deferring conscious scrutiny until later) connected to the latent contents of the dream. We might say that the method of free association set up the rails down which those trains of free thought could then travel. It was not simply that Freud saw free association as a part of the dream – extended in part by the sleep-like disposition of the free-associating analysand; he regarded free associations as *intrinsically interpretive*.

The meaning of the chains of ideas being articulated would not, of course, be clear to begin with. The analyst would have to be patient and remain quiet. However, this stoical stance – the analyst frozen in neutrality – was to become an unfortunate form of practice embodied by those analysts who were waiting for the rarefied returns of the repressed: those golden moments when a signifier seemed to tell it all, or when a slip of the tongue arrived as a divine unconscious intervention. In the beginning, in the truly classical era of psychoanalysis, the analyst remained quiet because he was deeply engaged in a mutual process in which both participants were facilitating a flow of ideas that would prove illuminating.

It is crucial to our understanding of the cases to follow, as well as to our appreciation of this particular form of Freudian practice, to realise that Freud was not waiting for singular moments but was unconsciously following many lines of thinking. In 'Studies on Hysteria' he gave us some insight into the psychic form of a line of thought:

> The logical chain corresponds not only to a zig-zag, twisted line, but rather to a ramifying system of lines and more particularly to a converging one. It contains nodal points at which two or more threads meet and thereafter proceed as one.[21]

The three cases in this book will help us to see how complicated a process this form of listening is. Freud tells us that comprehending any logical chain of thought means following a zig-zag. But what exactly does this mean? Because of the nature of the dream-work – condensation, displacement, substitution, composites, and so forth – any unconscious idea is going to travel through many different forms. It may be packed inside an image containing other ideas, displaced as an affect onto another 'innocent' thought, substituted by a stand-in, compromised by melding with another single object. To follow any logical chain means travelling along tracks that move through many different *forms* of representation. So, as an unconscious idea follows its sequential path, it moves in and out of various modes of articulation in order to complete itself.

Freud repeatedly used the metaphor of the weaver to illustrate what he meant by a zig-zagging line of thought. When discussing the dream of the botanical monograph he noted that the monograph was 'a regular nodal point in the dream' and that 'numerous trains of thought converged upon it' – so much so that we were now in a 'factory of thoughts where, as in the "weaver's masterpiece" . . . "Unseen the threads are knit together/And an infinite combination grows."'[22] (Here Freud quotes from Goethe's *Faust*, Part I.)

This form of speaking creates a tapestry of meaning obviously suited to unconscious thinking. And it is not difficult to see that free association is a form of creativity.

4

Listening

Freud repeatedly described the particular frame of mind that the psychoanalyst had to adopt when listening to the analysand's free associations. In 'On Beginning the Treatment' he wrote: 'while I am listening to the patient, I, too, give myself over to the current of my unconscious thoughts.'[23] In 'Recommendations to Physicians Practising Psycho-Analysis' he added:

> The rule for the doctor may be expressed: 'He should withhold all conscious influences from his capacity to attend, and give himself over completely to his "unconscious memory".' Or, to put it purely in terms of technique: 'He should simply listen, and not bother about whether he is keeping anything in mind.'[24]

In this listening position Freud is at pains to add that the analyst must adopt an attitude that is similar to the patient's. Neither is to think consciously about what is being said. Instead, in order to facilitate the flow of ideas, both participants must suspend their critical faculty and give themselves over to simply speaking and simply listening.

Ever the theoretician, however, Freud opts to put this relationship into his metapsychology:

> To put it in a formula: he must turn his own unconscious like a receptive organ towards the transmitting unconscious of the patient. He must adjust himself to the

patient as a telephone receiver is adjusted to
the transmitting microphone. Just as the receiver
converts back into sound waves the electric oscillations
in the telephone line which were set up by sound waves,
so the doctor's unconscious is able, from the derivatives
of the unconscious which are communicated to him, to
reconstruct that unconscious, which has determined
the patient's free associations.[25]

This is a startling passage and a very challenging one
to decipher. In the first place Freud situates the work of a
psychoanalysis unequivocally within unconscious intersubjectivity. Even though both participants are conscious, consciousness does not play a mediating role. But implicit in
Freud's theory is an obvious fact about consciousness itself:
however conscious we may be of a thought crossing our
mind, we are unconscious of the reasoning that links those
conscious contents over the course of time.

Consciousness, then, is driven by unconscious lines of
interest.

But Freud does not distinguish for his reader the particular type of unconscious thinking he is using in his
metaphor. It is certainly not the unconscious that operates
repression. Freud's term for this aspect of unconscious
work is that of a 'telephone receiver' and it is this latter
word, 'receiver', that I wish to emphasise.

In earlier essays I have distinguished between two
forms of unconscious work: reception and repression.[26] The
receptive unconscious or, to put it differently, unconscious
work that is engaged in reception, is the work that Freud
describes when he argues that the analyst 'receives' the
analysand's communications. If the analyst's unconscious
were operating in a mode of repression, then obviously he
or she would be unable to receive the analysand's unconscious messages in this way.

Of course, from time to time the analyst's unconscious
certainly does repress what he or she is hearing from the
analysand. Inevitably the analyst will be subject, too, to
other defences that will distort or interfere with what he
or she hears. But let us focus here on those unconscious

processes that are, for the most part, not the work of inter-
ference but the work of reception. If the work of repression
is built around the axis of the forbidding father (the name of
the father, the superego, the laws of socialisation that forbid
desire and aggression) then the work of reception derives
from the world of mutual communication between infant
and mother which forms the foundation of the unconscious
itself.

When Freud says that he can listen to a patient
through a receptive frame of mind, he can make this statement – which otherwise goes against his fundamental
theory of repression – because he is drawing on the object
relation which precedes the father's imposing laws that
demand self-deception from the child. By asking the patient
to adopt a sleep-like repose and to speak what he or she
thinks *without critical activity*, Freud returns the patient –
and himself – to the earliest form of relationship.

This primary repressed unconscious is not displaced by
secondary repression any more than the self's relation to
the maternal unconscious (on *its* terms) is displaced by the
arrival of the paternal unconscious and the laws (mental
structures) that begin to distort desires which had previously been free to roam the object world, according to the
pleasure principle. It is constructed over a long period of
time during which the infant and child form the codes of
their existence. One obvious example of such codification is
the way in which sounds form into the words that are part
of the system of language. But the way we are meant to be
– according to mother, father and others – and the ways we
are shaped relationally are also encoded in us, and we
express these codes in many subtle forms.

In *Poets Thinking*, Helen Vendler writes:

All poems, it seems to me, contain within themselves
implicit instructions concerning how they should be read.
These encoded instructions – housed in the sum of all the
forms in which a poem is cast, from the smallest phonetic
group to the largest philosophical set – ought to be
introduced as evidence for any offered interpretation.[27]

Vendler proceeds to argue that different poets will 'not resemble each other, that they will devise characteristic and recognizable patterns of thinking' so that 'each poet is so distinctive in patterns of mental expression.'[28]

In like manner, the free-associating analysand carries within his or her way of being, discourse, and manner of relating, 'implicit instructions' that communicate with the analyst's capacity for seeing 'recognisable patterns'. It will take time for the analyst to decode the analysand's free associations, but it will take place through the analyst's act of reception and translation. Indeed, Freud recognises that the role played by the work of reception is greater than that played by repression in the system unconscious.

In the sessions to follow we shall be impressed by the ways in which analysands pose implicit questions in the session and then work very hard to try to answer them, *unconsciously*. So too we shall see that the analysts are largely unaware of the collaboration in following certain lines of thought that characterise these quite ordinary sessions.

Why is this distinction so important?

Again, if we return to the history of psychoanalysis we can see that all theoretical schools adopted Freud's theory of repression and dropped his theory of reception. Instead of following the logic of sequence within the multiple lines of thought presented in a session, analysts opted to listen for derivatives of repressed material. They were, that is, engaged in a *selective listening* which unwittingly mirrored the selective activity of repression itself. By centring a theory of the unconscious so exclusively around the theory of repression, psychoanalysis thus came to enact the very defence it privileged. It became a repressive force, pushing out of the mind of both participants a much wider and deeper world of meaning.

In effect, the theory of repression – allowed to occupy sole place within the history of psychoanalysis as *the* theory of the unconscious – eliminated unconscious perception, unconscious organisation and unconscious communication from psychoanalytic theory. It was, and remains, a rather remarkable act of auto-castration.

Freud's dream-work theory offered psychoanalysis an understanding of how the subject nominates certain ordinary experiences of the day with psychic value, how those emotional experiences are then woven into the underlying movement of pre-existent ideas, and how through the dream all are brought together into some new reading that is latent within the sequence of the dream logic. A session, then, is an act of creation – a composition – that expresses the subject's daily interpretation of his or her existence.

both
pt + PA

Freud had grasped how the evenly suspended analyst can read the communications of the free-associating analys- and through an ordinary function of unconscious perception – the ability to discover patterns or, in the case of the speech, the logic of sequence. However, this was abandoned in favour of the repression model – and everything that did not accord with this model was relegated under the 'descriptive unconscious' signifier, which meant that it was lacking in the dynamic of sexuality and aggression.

o

Part of the aim of this book is to restore Freud's original understanding of unconscious thinking. In the next chapter we take a little more time to discuss the Freudian Pair.

repression model: another prop
in F: projection of Rank.

5

To catch the drift

Freud's most lucid account of how psychoanalysis works is to be found in his 1923 essay 'Two encyclopaedia articles'[29]. I have discussed this at length elsewhere[30] but I shall consider it again in brief because it is essential for the reader to have these important passages in mind when reading the cases that follow.

In the essay Freud assigned two tasks: one to the analysand, the other to the analyst. In effect, they are mental positions that each participant is asked to occupy in order for psychoanalysis to take place. I have termed their relationship and the task 'the Freudian Pair'.

First, Freud's instructions to the patient:

The treatment is begun by the patient being required to put himself in the position of an attentive and dispassionate self-observer, merely to read off all the time the surface of his consciousness, and on the one hand to make a duty of the most complete honesty while on the other not to hold back any idea from communication, even if (1) he feels that it is too disagreeable or if (2) he judges that it is nonsensical or (3) too unimportant or (4) irrelevant to what is being looked for. It is uniformly found that precisely those ideas which provoke these last-mentioned reactions are of particular value in discovering the forgotten material.[31]

Now Freud's instructions to the analyst:

Experience soon showed that the attitude which the analytic physician could most advantageously adopt was to surrender himself to his own unconscious mental activity, in a state of *evenly suspended attention*, to avoid so far as possible reflection and the construction of conscious expectations, not to try to fix anything he heard particularly in his memory, and by these means to catch the drift of the patient's unconscious with his own unconscious.[32]

It is noteworthy that Freud asks the analysand, in effect, to give up trying to be profound or even thoughtful and instead to say simply what crosses the mind. Similarly, the psychoanalyst is to do without memory or anticipation; instead, the analyst must give way to unconscious listening.

This is not to be selective listening: the analyst is to be without such desire. Compare this position with the view that the analyst should always observe the transference, or track the subject's slips of the tongue, or follow the opera of projection or projective identification. Such selectivity could be understood as a defence against the complexity of a session, whereas Freud's innovative method of listening honours this complexity and encourages the analyst to meet the analysand in an intermediate area in which they share something of the same frame of mind.

The issues of practice arising from this technique are demanding. In the first place, both participants have to give up the understandable wish to 'make sense' of what is being said as the session proceeds.

In abandoning reasoned thought in favour of associative thinking and speaking, both participants regress together. The ambient condition – one lying on a couch, the other sitting comfortably, free to stare off into the middle distance – the long stretches of silence, and the speakings without expecting a reply: all hark back to the early years of one's being. The difference, of course, is that since both participants are now intellectually adult, this is a return to a prior form of thinking equipped with more sophisticated unconscious capabilities, as well as more highly developed forms of consciousness.

Both patient and analyst know that however non-verbal the experience feels, both will be attempting to put into words retrospectively what they find they have been thinking. Consciousness will arrive, eventually, as a loaded after-thought: stocked and replete with the workings of the uncon-scious. Knowledge of this yield to come, from the growth of thought through the Freudian Pair, is deeply reassuring to both participants, who for long periods of time actually do not know what they mean by what they are saying.

But how does one judge an analysis like this?

It would certainly make no sense to ask an analyst in a supervision, for example, what he or she thinks is going on at any one point in time. If the psychoanalyst is immersed in the Freudian Pair he or she should not be able to answer this kind of question, unless of course the analyst has split off part of his or her personality under the demands of supervision to observe what he or she can from 'the out-side'. Analysts who are deeply immersed in their sessions do not know much of what is taking place.

Given this limitation, how can we judge the value of the work? How do we know if there *is* real work taking place, as opposed to no work at all?

In his theory of the dream day Freud argues that we all have vivid, intense experiences which, he claims, have a 'higher psychic value' than other experiences. The same is true for the analyst within a session. He or she will find, while listening to the patient's talkings, that certain con-tents are simply more *striking* than others. This may prompt the analyst either to repeat the word that seemed so valu-able, or to ask for further associations to the content.

If those interventions – which, it should be stressed, are not conscious interpretations – release further material that is more precise or detailed, then the supervisor of this kind of work can rest assured that analytical work is taking place. If such echoes of the content are not in unconscious rapport with the analysand's unconscious thinking, then the analysand either will not respond in detail or may resort to abstraction.

Abstraction by the patient may be an indication that the analyst has distracted the analysand's unconscious work; but, conversely, it may also suggest that the analyst has come to a core issue that meets with resistance. When a patient moves from *talking about* his or her life to *reflecting* on his or her life, this is very often a resistance to the analytical process itself – the analysand moves to abstract thinking as a defence against being a conduit for unconscious ideation.

In the background of the consciousnesses of both participants, however, is an underlying, unremitting question: 'What does this mean?' In the sessions with Arlene, Caroline and Annie we shall note the surprising number of occasions in which analysands ask questions, both explicit and implicit. What is even more striking is the evidence that such questioning seems to be the drive behind the process of thought itself – as if, from the infantile moment until the time we die, we are in a state of endless questioning about our lives.

Perhaps surprise is inherent in the traumatic but absorbing experience of having a mind. Mental life, in itself, endlessly takes the self unawares. One's mind – one's unconscious, in particular – is constantly picking up 'objects' in one's life (in the environment or in memory, through desire or anxiety) which raise doubts.

'In the daytime,' writes Freud in *The Interpretation of Dreams*, 'we drive shafts which follow along fresh chains of thought.' He explains that 'these shafts make contact with the intermediate thoughts and the dream-thoughts now at one point and now at another' and how 'in this manner fresh daytime material inserts itself into the interpretive chains'.[33] Vivid experiences in the here and now create lines of contact down into the flow of deep dream-thoughts that carry the history of the self and all its interests. That deep stream of thought is actually an interpretive chain.

So we have some clues as to why we ask questions.

Our mind, as a part of self experience, is curious in its own right and challenges the part of us delegated to think about what is in it. We are interpreting our lives all the time – in deep unconscious conceptualisations – and those understandings or convictions raise questions.

Why did I feel the way I did yesterday when talking to X? What did my response mean? Why did I elect to spend time with X rather than Y? And how does this change my relation to Y?

We will return in Chapter 11 to the conundrums posed by living within these sorts of questions, but at this stage it should be noted that it is an intrinsic part of the free-associative process. Indeed, as will become evident in the cases of Arlene, Caroline and Annie, questions seem to be the basis of human freedom. Free associations could not exist without curiosity; moreover, the capacity to free associate seems to be contingent on the existence of unsettling dilemmas.

6

Scoring the unconscious

In Chapters 7–9 we shall demonstrate how analysands who talk about whatever comes to mind are articulating lines of thought of which they are mostly unconscious. While the manifest topics will seem disconnected – how does talking about going to a shopping mall follow from discussing a novel by James Joyce? – listening to enough of these manifest meanderings reveals chains of ideas. This is the latent content not evident in the manifest text. It is the hidden discourse of the unconscious which speaks beneath the surface of articulated ideas; it is the connecting link between apparent verbal ramblings.

As we examine the sessions to follow, our main task will be to concentrate on this particular form of sequence. However, we must not forget that the chain of verbal thoughts is only one of many forms of sequence, each of which bears its own logical structure.

What about the sequence revealed through the tones of voice a person employs to give emphasis to his or her utterances? What about the way that person uses his or her body (hands, feet and, particularly, facial expression) to indicate a sequence of ideas? What about the rhetorical aims of the individual's speech, the way he or she persuades an other, even if that other is not present? Doesn't the rhetoric of presentation reveal a pattern that bears a logical ambition? What about the way a person structures his or her effect on the other – in this case, the analyst – in what is termed the transference? Isn't the transference, often revealed through presumptions about the character of the analyst–other, itself a logic of sequence that becomes discoverable progressively over time? What about the analyst's countertransference – that complex density of emotion, memory, received pressure from the patient's assumptions, and coercion by the patient's speech acts: does this not also reveal itself gradually as time goes on? Doesn't emotion – a 'moving experience' of affects, ideas, memories, desires, relational assumptions and situational states – only become understandable if and when its logic is progressively revealed? (Indeed, as a moving experience, it would have to move before we could know its character.)

These questions would seem to demand a typology for the unconscious. To respect the various forms of unconscious sequence we can construct different *categories* (the linguistic, the bodily, the sonic, the relational, and so on), each with sub-categories that we can term *orders*. So under the category of the relational we would find the orders of transference and countertransference. We might also want to include a separate order for what Winnicott termed 'interplay' between self and other. This is a sort of improvisational logic, something not revealed through narrative content but occurring in the play between self and other – something more like the spontaneity of jazz.

The visual category might include, for example, the imaginary and the dramatic orders, whilst the sonic category might comprise the orders of pitch, metre, rhythm, cadence and tone.

The linguistic category could include the separate orders of grammar, syntax, semantics, narrative logic, figures of speech, and so forth. If we take single words – or signifiers, as Lacanians term them – we discover sequential vectors implicit in both the sound and the sense of a single word, as well as in that word's usage within its linguistic and wider contexts. A word is a sound and it will sound like other words. Listening to someone talking, we will hear certain sounds repeated, others that are similar to one another, and some that constitute a kind of phonemic cluster. But words are not simply phonemic orders: they mean something. Speaking causes certain word associations to arise in the speaker and in the listener that will be contextually significant. That context can vary from the subtle terms of the individual relationship to the widespread field of the person's culture.

As we speak, therefore, words evoke clusters of ideas that will link with other clusters, themselves also moving along in sequence. So we see that even within the linguistic category alone – and if we focus just on the phonemic and semantic capability of words – we already have a thicket of meanings moving along in sequential time. If we add dimensions from the sonic category – stress, pitch, cadence, duration, silence – these lines of expression open up the field of unconscious expression even more widely, thickly and deeply.

Under the category of the body we would certainly want to include the order of the soma, to recognise a logical process occurring within the body. Indeed, the field of psycho-somatics or somato-psychics recognises that disruptive processes in the body (carcinogens, cardiac symptoms, and so on) proceed according to their own logic. Some might wish to exclude this order from the field of psychoanalysis – but this would be an egregious error, as the psychoanalyst is often the first clinician who is able to observe the nascent logic of a psychic issue moving into the soma.

There are also unconscious *positions*. The noteworthy positions developed by and for psychoanalysts include the libidinal positions (oral, anal, phallic, genital) and Klein's paranoid–schizoid and depressive positions. Such positions may cast the self's articulations within the momentary realm of a certain frame of mind. If at a certain moment no position is of particular significance, then one could say, following Hartmann, that it is in *neutral*.

Finally in our typology of unconscious sequence, there is *character*, the specific idiom of a person's being in the world. Character is deployed in discourse through the particular way (idiom) in which the person expresses himself or herself through the various categories and orders. But it is also dependent on the sensory skill of the other, through whom or upon whom a subject's character impresses itself.

The significant *elements* of psychic life (drives, affects, and so on) are thus articulated through the different orders, usually simultaneously.

Beyond the typology proposed above, there are also *unconscious structures*. Perhaps the most notable of these is the superego, a mental structure derived from thousands of intersubjective and intrasubjective engagements during the child's formative years. But there are also many other unconscious structures – an untold number of paradigms for being and relating that derive from the self's processional experience of the object world. (To 'experience' an object is to engage a process specific to that subject and that object.) Such structures – processional memories – will be expressed through the categories and orders of unconscious articulation.

To remind us that as we move through any day in our lives we express ourselves in all these different categories, we would benefit from an image which could help us keep in touch with the complexity of unconscious thought. In *The Freudian Moment* I proposed that we use the image of a symphonic score to help us imagine the simultaneous sequential movement of positions, elements, structures and character through the many categories and orders.[34] It also helps to illustrate the thickness, complexity and interconnectedness of unconscious thinking.

Where the staves of an orchestral score – stacked vertically – would show the 'lines of thought' for the violin part, say, or the tuba part, our score of the unconscious would have lines representing categories such as the linguistic, or the bodily, or the sonic. Moving from left to right we would 'read' the order of sequence of the unconscious, just as one would follow the unfolding of the music. The image therefore allows us to imagine the simultaneity of vertical and horizontal movement intrinsic to our articulation of unconscious ideas in distinctly different categories, so that they join up to form a kind of harmonisation of thought. A line of thought may be expressed, for example, linguistically, sonically, bodily and relationally all at the same time. The means of expression will be different, but each category will add its own form of thinking to the overall movement of the unconscious articulation.

The psychoanalyst – the student of unconscious life – works every day, for hours on end, at the intersection of the different logical sequences articulated by his or her analysands. It is possible to do this only because of the analyst's own unconscious reception to these forms of thought. And that receptivity is possible because the analyst's unconscious *knows* the different categories of thought and, further, knows how to listen to patterns of expression.

Naturally, analysts will vary considerably in what they hear and in what they follow. Sometimes it will be a single sonic line of thought. For example, in listening to one analysand describing her conflict with a neighbour, I heard the patient's tone shift when she uttered certain words: 'So, I said I thought it was right that he should be *billed* for the extra service he *wanted*.' I recognised by now – after several years of working with this analysand – that such words were spoken with a metallic voice, as if on an electronically recorded message. I understood this emphasis to indicate that while reproaching the other, the patient was at the same time backing away from an affective encounter by altering her personality. When I heard her speaking like this it was not a conscious act on my part to isolate this line of thought; it was a striking moment and it drew my attention. I would on occasion return to her words, speak them as best I could in her voice, and ask her to think about how she was withdrawing her feelings into a robotic self at that moment. While she had some difficulty at first in grasping this observation, it was not long before she could add emotional associations to such observations: 'Well, frankly, I wanted to kill him but I didn't know what to do, because I didn't want to give him the advantage of knowing what I was feeling.'

In like manner, a zig-zagging line of thought might be carried at one moment (or unit of expression) by a wave of the hand accompanied by a high vocal pitch, the next by a metaphor redolent with multiple meanings, and then by a sequence of ordinary observations that made sense as a further articulation of the idea being expressed by the analysand.

While I am proposing that we try to define the many categories and orders through which we could differentiate the various forms of unconscious articulation, I am not sure that even the most thorough effort would achieve such an aim. And although it might help us think about this highly complex picture, in the end the intelligence that we understand to be unconscious thinking cannot be reduced to such a typology. It runs the risk of creating a false impression, for in fact the unconscious mind does not ultimately operate according to separate systems of logic – it is all of a piece.

The image of a symphonic score does, however, help us to imagine the formal characteristics of unconscious thought and thus enables us to distinguish *category errors* that we often make when discussing clinical material. For example, the fact that the analysand is speaking through the transference does not preclude the possibility that at the very same time he or she is also articulating other ideas through narrative sequence, sonic language or body speech. The aim of this imaginary typology is to help the clinician to differentiate the various mental phenomena that occur simultaneously in a session, perhaps helping to prevent a confusion of theoretical tongues.

As you read the vignettes to follow, remember a few things.

First, more is left out of these reports and commentaries than is included. Something as simple, as basic, as the *sound* of these people's voices is eliminated from our consideration. That alone makes this act of representation a form of misrepresentation. I can justify this only on the grounds that I have given myself a limited brief. I want to provide samples of how analysands express themselves through that logic which was of special interest to Freud: the logic of narrative sequence.

Second, we leave out most of the analysand's past and history in order to protect the individual's identity. This is, of course, a necessity. But by leaving out the past we omit the real that has left indelible marks on the self.

Past and history are not the same thing. The past happened. It is composed of events that affected the self, some of which can be remembered, but most of which are outside memory altogether. History is a person's transformation of the past into a story which that person can tell himself or herself. Sometimes the story does indeed derive from the past, but even for the most sincere of analysands, his or her history will be more like a myth.

Third, bear in mind that the psychoanalysts who have graciously permitted the presentation of their work are at risk of the reader saying, 'But why didn't you say this?' or, 'But don't you see what you left out of your consideration?' And it is inevitable that the experienced reader will wonder why certain issues were not 'taken up' in the hour. So let us be reminded that these are samples of work in progress and that no one session can or should attempt to address all those issues that seem to be moving within an hour. Indeed, as I discussed in Chapter 5, a good analysis is one in which the analyst is so lost in the process that he or she will not be very skilled at answering questions about why he or she said a certain thing, and not something else that might seem to the observer to be crying out for articulation. As I hope is clear by now, it is impossible to follow all the lines of thought being articulated. And that includes those that are 'close to the surface' – that is, ones we believe we *can* track. If we think about those lines of thought that are deeper, or those that are latent and not active in the reported session – like the horn section remaining silent for a while in a Bruckner symphony – then we are humbled by the fact that the *overwhelming amount* of unconscious thinking is entirely outside of consciousness.

We can perhaps be sympathetic to those analysts who jump in and claim knowledge about what is 'really going on' in an hour. After all, it is a hard place to be, the psycho-analytical position. You do not get to know much – and yet you are surrounded by the movement of meaning. But if we empathise with the need to 'know' in the midst of the overwhelming complexity of mental expression, then we must at the same time be highly wary of any psychoanalyst, or group of analysts, who claim to have found a way to decode *the* unconscious.

Freud's advice, that in the state of evenly suspended attentiveness the analyst should 'catch the drift of the patient's unconscious with his own unconscious', is not merely sound – it is vital. This means, however, that although we do gain unconscious understandings of the movement of our analysand's unconscious life, such knowledge will only rarely enter our own consciousness. So as conscious beings, we are rather asleep. What we learn, we discover when we are not awake. We live with our patients, unconscious to unconscious.

Before reading the sessions that follow in the main text, please refer to the appendix, where you will find the sessions presented without commentary. It will be most helpful to read them through first in this form. Try to follow Freud's advice. Do not try to figure out 'what is going on' or what the analysands mean by what they say. In each case, just relax and read the session. Even better, read it again, even a third time. See if you discover a pattern of thought that reveals itself to you over time. What have you learned from the analysand's unconscious? Try to avoid importing your favourite selective analytical facts, such as dissociations, drive derivatives, the castration complex, the transference, or the ego position. That can come later.

After you have read through the sessions in this way, I recommend that you then read the cases together with their commentaries, in Chapters 7–9.

Finally, we note the irony of this moment. Having argued that an analyst, in a state of *evenly suspended attentiveness*, is largely unconscious of what his analysand 'means', you are about to read my commentaries which deconstruct these sessions in considerable detail. This intellection does not reflect the *in situ* work of the psychoanalyst, but illustrates the review work of a 'supervisor'. I have studied these sessions several times before writing the commentary solely to point out the subtle forms of unconscious expression that would otherwise elude the working analyst immersed in the task of unconscious thinking.

7

'Arlene'

Arlene is in her mid-thirties. She moved with her parents from Greece to England when she was three. Soon after their arrival in Leeds her sister was born, and when Arlene was five the parents took in her first cousin, who was almost deaf and who communicated through signing. Arlene's parents were hard-working people who intended to open a hotel. To this end, her mother spent many hours away studying English and hotel management, while her father worked in a restaurant in another town. Following their move to England, Arlene's mother decided that the family should speak only in English, and the Greek language was for the most part banished.

Gradually the parents began to live apart, although they did not divorce during Arlene's childhood. They put their money into a hotel, which was run by Arlene's mother and her extended family (some of whom had been living in Leeds before their arrival, with others joining them from Greece).

Arlene teaches piano to children in local schools. She studied music at university and has continually supplemented her musical education since then. She is a member of a small female choir that hires rehearsal rooms at the local Conservatory of Music, and occasionally they employ a member of the teaching staff to help them improve their skills. Arlene's choir had recently come under pressure to use a voice teacher who was overbearing, and the session below refers to the choir's decision to insist that this teacher no longer be associated with them.

The day before the session Arlene had tried several times to call her psychoanalyst, in order to confirm that she would be attending the session. She had been away and had not been sure she would be back in time for her analysis. The analyst's phone was operational but her answerphone did not 'pick up' after the customary number of rings, so Arlene hung up, thinking she had dialled the wrong number or that the phone was not working. After several attempts, however, the answerphone finally kicked in and she let the analyst know that she would be coming to the session as planned.

Analyst is a woman

Arlene comes through the door and greets the analyst. She says that she tried calling several times the previous day but the phone did not seem to work. She asks if there was something wrong with the phone, as it did not pick up. She says that perhaps she didn't 'persist' long enough, as eventually it turned out fine. She goes into the room and lies on the couch. There is a short silence.

The patient begins with a question that might be put as follows: 'Why did the other not come when I called?' The free-associative answer appears to be, first, that perhaps there is something wrong with the means of communication (the phone), and then 'perhaps I didn't persist long enough'.

Analyst:
The incident with the phone seems a follow-on from our last session: how can one be heard?

The analyst refers to the previous session (three days earlier), which was taken up with Arlene feeling that she was not being heard, so today's session continues the questioning.

Arlene:
(nods and then speaks slowly)
Yesterday . . . our choir went to the president of the Conservatory and talked to her. Because every girl in the group has a problem with the voice teacher. And she gave in at last, and we are allowed now to sing alone, without the voice teacher, every Sunday night. *(pauses)* As our choir met yesterday, they said that I should be the one who should do the talking. *(pauses)* It was very

A voice teacher is someone meant to improve the vocal means of communication. She is sacked by the group. What does it mean to Arlene to get rid of the person in charge of the verbal medium? (See the discussion below.)

The patient's free association is to the group picking her to speak, but Arlene wonders why it is that she finds such a task difficult. She answers that she does not like conflict and tries to avoid it. She will not answer back even if someone

opinion. I cannot come up with one. So if somebody says to me something then I take it for granted that it is so. And actually, in my profession this is risky because you do have to hold your position. You don't say to the other person, actually what you say seems very sensible and I agree with you.

Analyst:
What if you do say what you think?

Arlene:
Well, if I do not comply, then I make everything much worse. That is my thought. *(pauses)* I don't know where that comes from. My mother has been saying it to me all the time: anybody can come and you will follow him . . . But I somehow think that my mother talked me into it for so long that I came to believe it myself.

The analyst asks a question and Arlene replies spontaneously: if I speak, I will make matters worse. What kind of 'matters' is not clear.
 She says that she does not know where this comes from, but then recalls her mother's identification of her. Ironically, the mother's observation is a maternal enactment, 'you must follow what I say', and the child fulfils the maternal wish. So recalling the previous question – 'why do I not have "my own position"?' – Arlene replies that her mother has it for her.

+ holds it away from her

Analyst:
That is an interesting insight.

The analyst acknowledges that this is an important insight derived, of course, from the analysand's own process of thought.

Another silence of four minutes follows.

The analyst felt that at first the silence was Arlene now absorbed inside the mother. Her silence expressed the absence of her own voice. Then the analyst felt the text(ure) of the silence changed – this became more *a silence observed.* After a while the analyst found herself speaking.

Analyst:
So this has been your way of avoiding conflict in your life?

Arlene:
Yes, as long as I remember I have been like this.

Analyst:
You are thinking . . . ?

Arlene:
As a little child I would avoid conflicts of all kinds. I did not quarrel with other kids. I wasn't aggressive and I did not defend myself.

A short silence ensues before Arlene continues.

That is not strictly true. I would give an opinion, but if someone said something else I would not oppose it. I just don't know where that comes from. My sister can do it much better. I think I just did not develop in some ways after I was a child, but I don't know. My sister was outspoken.

The patient re-poses the question. Why, if she spoke her opinion and then someone 'said something else', did she not 'oppose' – i.e. not speak? She effectively poses another question – 'I just don't know where that comes from' – but then she thinks of her sister. So we can put it like this: 'Why is it that I can speak once, but not again? Because if my sister came along and spoke then I could not oppose her, so I remained silent.' The sub-theme here is of a sibling interruption that breaks Arlene's will to speak. She can speak 'once' – that is, she must be the only child-speaker. If others are around she refuses to engage in sibling competition. In that respect, her sister could be outspoken, while Arlene silenced herself.

Analyst:
You have asked where the 'you' that speaks just once came from, and you follow it through with thoughts about your sister. After her arrival, I expect you felt gutted. You did not feel like talking.

The analyst makes the simple but incrementally important link between associations.

Arlene:

Um . . . *(pauses)* She is stronger than I am. She was able to work with my cousin. At the age of five or six I wasn't spoken to because my mother was never there and my father didn't bother with me anyway. There were always guests in the hotel, always needing my parents. And my mother never spoke with me. When we moved out of our first flat, we lived for a short while in a large hotel. My mother was gone the whole day long, even in the evenings . . . She went to the English Institute to improve her English so that she and my father could open their own hotel. And I remember that my sister was occupied with my cousin . . . and I couldn't communicate with her at that time because I didn't sign. She was nearly deaf and my sister could speak to her by signing. I couldn't speak the deaf language.

Analyst:

You did not speak the deaf language.

Arlene:

No, I don't know why.

Analyst:

Well, you may have a theory. Following the line of your thought, your mother did not talk to you and so perhaps you thought that there was no point in speaking to someone who was deaf to your presence.

Arlene:

I had not thought of it that way, but I see what you mean.

Arlene replies by association. Her sister could speak and she could not. (See the discussion below.) She says that from five to six she wasn't spoken to because the mother was not there and the father did not speak. Guests (a group of rivals) successfully competed for the mother's attention. Arlene repeats the comment about the mother: 'my mother never spoke with me.'

She associates to not being able to speak to her cousin because she could not sign for the hearing-impaired. So in answer to the question, the rivalry with the sister follows the mother's rejections. Her inability to 'sign' with the deaf would be a derivative of her inability to speak to the mother who had deaf ears.

Prompted by Arlene's statement 'I don't know why', which the analyst takes as a wish to know, the analyst puts together what she has understood from the free associations.

Analyst:
I believe I have followed what
you've said, but you might want to
correct me.

Arlene:
No. I see that these are in fact my
thoughts, but just thinking out loud
I wasn't thinking. I mean, I didn't
know what it means.

Analyst:
That happens a lot in this room.

Arlene:
I am remembering my early
school years. Neither of my
parents asked . . . how is it in
kindergarten, or do you have
friends, or how is it with the
English children . . . And I still
remember the only incident where
my mother did something with me
alone . . . I was eight or nine years
old and she read excerpts from a
story about a girl who fell in love
with a boy who spurned her, and
later, when he was in love with
her, it was too late. I didn't
understand many things. She
should have noticed from the way
I spoke Greek. And it is at any
rate a very difficult passage. She
should have understood that I
couldn't understand it. And it was
really the only thing that my
mother ever did with me.

There is silence for two minutes.

Analyst:
The girl and the boy missed each
other.

Arlene:
Yes.

Comments such as this mitigate the
over-*transferisation* of analysis.
Pointing out that the analyst has
learned from the patient lessens the
toxic process of an over-transferised
discourse.

*Chilly: Does not allow agony of
not knowing what one says.*

This is common in the analytic
process. It is not a rarefied or unusual
moment.

Arlene recalls 'the only incident'
where her mother 'did something
with me alone'. It was reading
excerpts from the tale of a failed
romance. Question: 'Why did mother
read me this story?' Answer: 'Because
it is the story of loving someone who
does not listen and then later, when
it is too late and you no longer love
her, her love is not returned.' (A
theme of the analysis has been her
anger towards her mother, whom she
treats coldly.)
     Note that the mother does not
ask her questions in English about
everyday life, and the memory is of
her mother interrogating her in
Greek. We will return to this in the
discussion.

Analyst:

Like . . . ?

as if emotion connects →

Arlene:

My mother and I. *(she cries)* I think
the move separated us. Then my
sister was born. And then my
mother and father fell out with one
another.

Analyst:

Which made matters worse for you.

Arlene:

I don't think my mother ever
explained anything to me. She
indicated that she should not feel
obliged to explain things. For
example, the story she told me . . .
She would say: 'At this age you
should be able to speak it, your
Greek is enough. What is wrong
with you?'

*Another silence of four minutes
follows before Arlene continues.*

I can remember when my father
went to this other town to do
catering. Each Sunday when he
returned home to Leeds I said I
didn't want to go to school the next
day, so I could spend a day with
him because he was in Leeds on
Mondays. I pretended to have these
headaches. I did the same thing
with my mother. I would tell her I
wasn't feeling well so that when
she was around I could stay with

The analyst reports that Arlene
conveyed an emergent anguish,
— through a thick sound in her voice, so
the analyst asked along the affect
line of articulation.

As she experiences the emotion of
this loss of her mother Arlene is able
to immediately connect the move,
their separation *and then* the birth of
her sister, followed by the rift
between the parents. The analysand
instructs us as to the order of priority
through *the logic of her sequence.*
What competed with her mother?
The move first, then the separation,
then the birth of her sister and then
the parental separation.   *4 things*

The analysand's free association takes
her to the mother's verbal absence.
And from mother's absence to
Arlene's failure to remember her
mother tongue, Greek. So Arlene is
revealing here her introjective
identification of a maternal
projective identification. But the
mother's question, 'What is wrong
with you?', rings in the session as a
new question for the analysis.

The analyst felt that Arlene's silence
carried the affect of the mother's
question. It created silence and
speechlessness.   *Silence = being wrong*

Emerging from the silence
following the mother's question,
'What is wrong with you?', Arlene
free associates to her father being
away. One answer to the question
then is: 'I am distressed because my
father is away.' Loss of the ability to
speak Greek is therefore linked
with loss of the father. But soon
after mentioning the absent father,
Arlene *adds* the loss of her mother,
so the maternal question, 'What is

her. Then he stayed in this other town and rarely came home.

Analyst:
It was very painful to have been left by each of them. I think you must have felt quite lost.

Arlene:
Yes.

Analyst:
So you complied. You obviously felt you could not say that you wanted to go to the other town to stay with your father?

Arlene:
I think I lacked the courage. My mother always said he was so bad, so that she would say, 'What? You want to stay with your horrid father?'

Analyst:
And you must have been afraid she would say that she would have nothing further to do with you.

Another silence of three minutes follows.

Arlene:
My sister told me recently that I was left alone very often as a child. She remembered it very well . . . Even when my mother was present, she was so involved in her own things that she didn't talk, she didn't say anything.

There is a silence of two minutes before Arlene continues.

wrong with you?', continues to spring further answers.

Given the mental pain moving along with these associations, the analyst elects to follow the emotional experience that is unfolding. She emphasises the feelings present in the analysand. When Arlene replied, 'Yes', it was, reported the analyst, a deeply sad reply. A single, ordinary word carrying an entire emotional set.

Arlene changed her voice to that of the mother, and the analyst could feel a chill go up her spine. It was as if the mother was in the room. This is an articulation through the orders of identification and voice, a convergence of the relational and sonic categories.

This analyst did not know, at the time, why she said this, but on reflection we may see that as *she* felt afraid of the sound of the mother's voice, she spoke up for Arlene's affective experience.

This silence felt to the analyst as if Arlene was trying to recover from the depth of feeling.

The analyst felt that Arlene's move to her sister's recollections resulted from a need for Arlene to turn to recollective rather than affective memory.

We may wonder if *this* silence is an identification with the mother who does not speak. Once again, Arlene merges with the mother, combining narrative content with enactment.

My mother was so intimidating.

Now she lets us know why she merges with the mother. It is too frightening to be a differentiated *Yes* other.

Analyst:
Do you suppose this answers something of the riddle you have been thinking of in this session? Of wondering why you say something just once and not again, because you do not want conflict, and hope problems will just solve themselves?

The silence has allowed the analyst to reflect on the flow of associations. The pattern of associations came together in her mind in the form of this interpretation, which seems to answer the riddle posed by the patient.

Arlene:
I think that is right. In fact, at the time, when mother would yell at me, I would feel or say – or both – 'Well, that's it: you said it, but nothing will happen.' I was afraid of her. I did not want to make conflict. But . . .

Arlene qualifies our speculations about 'only once'. In this context she recalls a moment's despair as a child. Whatever she might hope for, if she asked her mother for something, nothing would happen. The idea that one only speaks once might therefore have been a resolution that she *a vow* would not ask the mother again and again.

Arlene pauses and then stirs on the couch.

The body speaks.

Well, after a while I did see my father. My mother forbade it, but I found a way and so did he and so we did manage.

Thus SKS' use of the word

Analyst:
Ah. So that's persistence! You persisted in telephoning, you persisted in pursuing your father, so you have a quiet belief that persistence is the thing, which must have been there when you insisted to the president of the Conservatory that the choir did not need a voice teacher.

The analyst makes a link to the healthy side of the analysand *who does persist*, unlike the part of her that she thinks gives up and seeks a solution only once. The analyst also indicates the work of the unconscious, pointing out how Arlene answers a question posed at the very beginning of the session.

He assumes persistence is good, can lead to more contact

Arlene:
Yes. I suppose that is right.

Analyst:
Um.

*Arlene stands up, greets the analyst
with a smile and a handshake, and
leaves.*

Discussion

We shall return now to a riddle deferred to this point.
Recall that Arlene associated to three ways of trying to
solve a problem: persistence; hope that the problem will
solve itself; and saying something once and then not again.
The sequence indicates psycho-development in reverse
order, from maturity (persistence), to the hopeful Oedipal
child, back to the infant who thinks omnipotently. By
indicating to the analysand how she persists, the analyst
points to Arlene's higher-level functioning, and she also
sustains her own analytic alliance with the healthy parts of
her patient, thus aligning herself with Arlene's life
instincts and the maturational process.

As we have seen, Arlene poses several questions to
herself as the session progresses. She begins by wondering
if she persisted long enough in phoning the analyst and
raises a question about whether she persists long enough in
life. There are many subsequent lines of thought that arise,
but at the end of the session, when she recollects that in
spite of her mother's threats she persisted in reaching her
father, she answers one part of the question.

The session *itself*, however, is an act of persistence.
Between the beginning of the session and the end, when
the question is answered, Arlene faces many obstacles. She
is confronted by a part of herself that is intimidated by
having to be the spokesperson for an overbearing voice
teacher at the Conservatory. Although she says that she
believes she speaks only once and not again, just after
narrating her story about the Conservatory she says that

with some people you have to persist 'for a very, very, very long time'. The repetition of 'very' is overdetermined. In this way, Arlene compromises between the notion that she speaks only once and the persistent side of her nature.

The repetition of a single word is a speech act that articulates another line of thought. This leads Arlene to think that she cannot oppose someone and might take on the other's opposing argument because she is so weak. Midway through the session, however, Arlene recalls her mother telling her that she would follow anyone – and *now* she is on the way to answering her question through the process of free association. The logic of sequence leads her to a mother who tells her she follows anyone and thus creates a myth that Arlene is weak and disinclined to stand her ground. The session ends with Arlene defying her mother to reach her father.

The analyst also noted an important moment of confusion. In narrating why she found what her mother said to her at eight or nine disturbing, Arlene had not yet indicated that the problem had to do with the mother speaking Greek. This confusion is articulated in the relational category, according to the communication between two orders – the transferential and countertransferential – that follow their own lines of thought. The confusion was too brief to become the basis of an analytical comment, but it was striking enough to reside within the analyst as a lingering after-effect. It is interesting to consider how such moments are *micro-traumas* in which the analyst is somewhat shocked by something said by the analysand yet, as with the child, the affect is deferred until sometime in the future when it will show up linked to a more obvious disturbance.

The movement into the relational category, as part of the flow of associations, is significant. It brings the analyst into Arlene's experience as a child. It is immediately after this that the analyst makes interpretations of the boy and girl missing one another, a comment that is simultaneously true about the content of the ideas being expressed and the relational experience constituted in the moment. This deepening of the session – an inevitable outcome when different orders of articulation are used simultaneously to express the same idea – leads Arlene to a powerful emotional experience. Hitherto a rather tough person, obviously trying to keep her feelings at bay, she is moved by the analyst's comment and she cries.

At this point it will not have been only the analyst's words that moved Arlene, but the *position* from which the analyst spoke (Arlene's position as a child of eight or nine) and the *way* the analyst used her voice. The human voice, an order of meaning within the sonic category, conveys feeling. The analyst's voice receives the nascent affect within Arlene.

We may note here that Arlene had missed the sound of the analyst's voice on the answerphone. What was wrong with the medium? She then talked about the vocalisation (the correct pronunciation) of Greek by her mother. She had discussed, prior to that, sacking the voice teacher. So we may follow a line of thought that goes like this: 'I find my mother's response to my voice traumatic as I do not speak in the way she demands, and I must rid myself of this intrusion into my inner world.' The analyst, however, is unconsciously attentive to the affects carried by Arlene's vocalisations – and her own vocal reply carried within it, no doubt, an articulation of empathic feelings for Arlene's position, in strong contrast to the mother who failed to do so. Thus one theme – 'I must get rid of bad media of communication' – is both articulated unconsciously and corrected in the way patient and analyst talk to one another.

The correction takes place in the relational category within the order that Winnicott termed the interplay between analyst and analysand. It is in the realm of their mutual engagement with one another, in the way they speak to and hear from the other, that a good medium for self–other interplay is established.

To the implicit question 'Why did I not speak to the deaf cousin?' the analyst has picked up a line of thought – that the mother was deaf to Arlene's presence – and an important unconscious link is made conscious. Throughout the session, however, there are silences that speak. Arlene does not go deaf, but she is not speaking – something that was true of her cousin who did not speak, but who signed. The analyst reported that no two silences felt the same; she also felt that Arlene's silence constituted an important voice. In the commentary we considered how we are silent (not obliged to speak) when we are infants. That is one line of thought which continued in the sessions following the one discussed here.

At the same time, however, silence may be a form of — defiance. The line of thought which maintains that 'I will only speak once' can be seen in the session in different forms: Arlene actually says that she will speak only once; *yes* she refuses to engage in competitive situations with others; she complains about having to speak for the group, yet she was the elected leader who confronted the president of the Conservatory. This line also converges at the end of the session where she defies her mother by speaking with her father. It would be some months following this session before these other lines of thought would enter the chain of associations in a way that made them fruitfully discussable. Arlene eventually saw how her 'I only speak once' was an omnipotent demand that the world follow her command. At the same time, however, it is a verbal signifier pointing to the thoughts of an infant, as if Arlene says, 'My deep loyalties are to my toddler self and with those convictions — when I felt real to myself.' So her omnipotence requests a sentient deconstruction of its silent logic.

What did I mean in the commentary by writing that Arlene's association 'I don't answer back' could be a transference line of thought, but that it existed in a wider context and should not be interpreted? Certainly we see many moments in the session that indicate how the analysand *may* be thinking transferentially and how, for example, her many silences following the analyst's comments could be ways of not answering back. Perhaps the answer is already clear. By being allowed to continue to speak without being organised into a transference interpretation, Arlene is able to elaborate her initial questions and to work on them; that is, to think further. The analyst felt this was the case even though she heard the transference. In another session, at another time, if she felt that Arlene was referring to the analyst, or enacting something

The PA allowes herself to abandon the pt
in silence by justifying her own silence as "good"

with the analyst that would benefit by entering consciousness," she would not have hesitated to interpret it.

Let us now follow another line of thought in this session. After talking about speaking up for the choir to the president of the Conservatory, Arlene asks a question: 'I don't know why, but even if someone understands that a person has a problem talking then people want exactly this person to do the talking.' After this she is silent for three or four minutes. Then she says, 'This was the same as with my parents,' and she proceeds to link this with the president of the Conservatory. This line of thought, however, must wait some time in the session before it is elaborated. She recalls her mother reading her a story in Greek and asking her questions. She felt that her mother should have understood that she had trouble understanding Greek but, even so, the mother insisted she do the talking. So the question 'Why am I asked to talk when I have a problem talking?' links to talking Greek with the mother who insists that the daughter proceed nonetheless. The analyst elects to focus on the difficulty of talking to a mother who is deaf to her words, an important theme that in many respects takes priority over my own observation here.

We may see that the question raised by the analysand is redolent with potential meanings that were no doubt explored and elaborated in later sessions. To take just one aspect of this complex question: what does it mean that Arlene recalls the moment when the mother was reading to her in Greek? This was the language they spoke before the move to England, when Arlene was their only child. The story the mother reads is of a failed love relation, but by speaking it in Greek – which her child is reproached for not understanding – the mother unconsciously informs the child that the reason the love relation failed was that the move broke up their language, shared home, culture and intimacy. The reproach may actually be that the child should have retained her Greek in order to speak it with the mother later, a mirror of the very story she is reading: what was once a possibility is no longer a possibility for those who could have been in love. Is the mother even reproaching the daughter for her failure to retain the

LH A – her mother's language, country –

mother's attachment to her country and language of origin? Is Arlene, therefore, the container of an *unspeakable* loss that she unconsciously articulates through the silences that punctuate her narrative? These and many more questions arrive out of this one single memory.

We may return within this question to another part of the session. We noted a contradiction that we took to be a riddle. People expected Arlene to talk. The president of the Conservatory really did not listen to Arlene when she talked. How were we to understand the link between these two points: (1) talk even if you do not want to; and (2) if you talk, we do not listen? We may now say that the one who does not want to talk is the Greek-speaking Arlene, who cannot remember her mother tongue and for whom speaking Greek is too difficult. This is the speaker the mother wants to hear. But when Arlene does talk to the mother, she speaks in English. This is not the speaker the mother wants to hear. So if Arlene is asked to speak in Greek she does not want to speak, and if she speaks in English she is not heard.

Arlene's position is in stark contrast to her sister's. While Arlene's early lingual relation with the mother was through Greek, her sister learned and spoke English with the mother. After Arlene has established that she did not quarrel with other children (which would include her sister), she says her sister was 'outspoken', and further that 'she is stronger' than Arlene. But the context of the free associations helps us to see why and in what way the sister is stronger. The Greek language (and Greece itself) is in the background of this family, but no one speaks the mother tongue. The sister is outspoken in English, perhaps to the delight of the mother – it is the sister who represents access to her new country. The sister is the child of the future, Arlene the child of the past. When Arlene does speak English it is of no significance to the mother, who unconsciously wants her to remain her Greek daughter.

Arlene's memory of the one time the mother showed her attention, when she was eight or nine, is obviously a screen memory. Let us concentrate on one word in her account. She discussed how difficult it was to understand something her mother was reading to her, saying that she was rebuked for this. It was 'a very difficult passage' and her mother 'should have understood that I couldn't understand it'.

What might have happened if the analyst had simply echoed the word 'passage'? Would the patient have understood that one passage she is referring to is the transition from Greece to England? Is this not the passage that the mother did not understand and could not explain to her daughter? And when she says of this supposedly literary moment, 'it was really the only thing that my mother ever did with me', is it not possible that the passage that she and her mother shared was this difficult transition from Greece to England? In this light, as discussed, Arlene is the daughter who must hold the mother's split-off loss, anguish, anxiety, depression and anger over having to leave her native land. But the word 'passage' also contains two other words that carry Arlene's meaning. One meaning of the word 'pass' is to defer a question or an issue: to pass over something. Arlene is the daughter who was passed over. The word 'age' may bear a meaning: that part of Arlene's coming of age included the trauma of losing her mother too soon; indeed, of leaving loving parts of herself and her mother in the early years of her life, in Greece.

Do we know for sure that Arlene unconsciously selects 'passage' because it bears these meanings? Of course not. But we take into consideration that in referring to the part of the story that was difficult for Arlene to understand in Greek, or to translate into English, Arlene could have said it was 'a difficult section' or 'a difficult part' or 'a difficult paragraph'. The point is that by electing the word 'passage' the analysand unconsciously articulates far more about her inner experience than she could have through these other possible wordings. Typically signifiers refer to other signifiers, establishing, as Lacan shows, the voice of the subject who speaks through these linked sounds. If the analyst receives the potential meaning of a word that bears other signifiers and if she sounds those words *spontaneously* then the analyst's unconscious responds to the patient's unconscious in a dialogue of signifiers.

This is one of the many ways in which unconscious communicates to unconscious. And importantly it is *creative*. So in the end, 'passage' may also yield the sound 'sage', as patient and analyst hear the wisdom of a self who knows what it means to pass through early trauma, to lose her voice, and to recover it many years later as she becomes part of a choir. The word 'choir' itself bears the sound of other signifiers: 'cry' and 'or'. You can cry or you can move on. And in many ways Arlene does move on, although she still needs to bring the affect linked to early trauma into a human relationship. So analyst and analysand will hear the song of the self together, they will be attuned to it, and in assembling the many voices of the past they constitute and hear from Arlene's inner choir.

Let us think further about Arlene and her mother. We may speculate that inside this complex bind is the daughter's refusal to fulfil her mother's link to Greece, even though it represents a time when Arlene had the mother to herself. For Arlene what is important is that once they moved to Leeds the mother no longer listened to her. That is, the mother to whom she wishes to speak, not the mother of the past, who is now gone.

This session reveals how a psychoanalyst should follow the chain of ideas presented, rather than picking up themes which may seem (perhaps correctly) to be immediately evident. It would have been possible quite early on for the analyst to have said something like: 'It is interesting that you say you only speak once, but actually you spoke up for the group with the president of the Conservatory, so you are more powerful than you would like to appear.' However accurate that comment might be, at that stage in the session it had not been adequately pursued by the analysand's own free associations. Further, given what we subsequently understand, it is more likely that the self who speaks only once is the toddler who spoke only in Greek and then not again. It is obviously not literally true that Arlene spoke only once, but she is referring to a language in which speaking felt more real to her once (upon a time). This was the only language emotionally relevant to herself and her mother, all the more saddening because the language is now lost. So when Arlene says she speaks 'only once' we may conjecture that she refers to a context in which this was psychically, if not actually, the case. This word, 'once', also bears another word within its sonic significance: we can hear the word 'one'. So when Arlene says that she was only spoken to once, we might conjecture that she means she could only be the object of maternal discourse when she was one – the only child. These two words, then, 'once' and 'one', converge to emphasise the significance of the bliss and the tragedy of being the one who was spoken to, not simply once, but as the only one – and once upon a time, when the mother could speak to her child.

Thus the story the mother tells of a failed romance is mirrored in the language of the telling. In the beginning the daughter loved the Greek-speaking mother, but the mother was preoccupied with other matters. The daughter then moves on – as she must – but she forgets her Greek. Later, the mother recalls her daughter, and tries to engage her in a love of speaking Greek. But the daughter has lost her connection to her mother tongue. It is too late. She cannot *now* translate Greek into English; that is to say, her Greek into her English self.

The rule of *following* as best one can the analysand's free associations is crucial to the patient's developing relationship to her unconscious. For it is crucial that Arlene sees how her own unconscious answers the question, 'Why do I feel I do not persist enough?' If this is the ordinary benchmark of analytical work, if these links are made conscious hundreds of times over the early months of an analysis, the analysand's conscious mind is gradually introduced to her own forms of unconsciousness.

It is by no means easy.

Every analysand is resistant to this new object relation. The idea that we are thinking and expressing ourselves unconsciously, all the time, is quite difficult for our consciousness to swallow. In part, this has to do with the issues Freud pointed to at the very beginning of psychoanalysis. Unconscious lines of thought will indeed reveal hidden sexual and aggressive ideas that are not acceptable to the self. They will also reveal those defences and forms of self-deception typical of the individual, and, as the literature of

cold rule

The rule of following robs the pt of the PA's wisdom.
The PA justifies this coldly: That's the only way you'll ever learn from your alone

ego psychology has illuminated, bringing these forms of defence to consciousness meets with resistance.

In our time, the beginning of the twenty-first century, there is a deep cultural contempt in Western societies for the idea, let alone the expressions, of the unconscious mind. Introducing any analysand to this aspect of the way we think and express ourselves is difficult indeed. But if the analyst goes about the work of illustrating *how the patient's mind* (not the analyst's mind) made the links in the free-associative chain of ideas, then the "evidence" is placed before the patient's consciousness for consideration.

In the session we have looked at there was one important sequence that the psychoanalyst did not follow up. Arlene recalls her mother asking 'What is wrong with you?' before going silent for several minutes. Next Arlene says, 'I can remember when my father went to this other town to do catering.' In a moment like this – and every analysis is replete with thousands of these *latent* connections – the analyst need only say something like, 'Your mother asks what is wrong with you, and after a long silence you reply that what is wrong is that your father is away.' This enables the analysand to see that this is *her* link.

Is this the truth, the whole truth, and nothing but the truth?

No.

As we see in this session there will be other lines of thought, some of which will converge to a nodal point and continue together (as when narrative, relational, affective and sonic lines converge to combine categories in expressing a core point). Others will reappear in later sessions to create other truths. By following the links made by the analysand, the analyst recognises the analysand's psychic reality as the author of the sessions and, as importantly, she indicates evidence of unconscious thinking.

We shall return to this issue in the last part of the book, but as we read through these sessions – evidence for the assertions to follow – it is important to observe how the analysands pose questions, answer them at the time, then pose new questions which in turn are answered in context, and so it goes on. A single question – 'Do I persist enough?'

Yes, one is condemned to only one's own authorship.
That is the bitter medicine the PA says one must swallow.

– may recur again and again in an analysis. Each questioning may spring entirely new sets of answers.

No analyst could possibly hear all of these questions, much less discover the answers articulated by the analysand. The entire point of Freud's theory of evenly suspended attentiveness, discussed earlier in this book, is that the analyst should *be unconscious* while listening to the analysand. There are, however, evocative moments in every session, and *explicit questions* always spring some kind of answer. Analysts trained in listening to free associations are alerted by an explicit question, knowing that the very next association will often, though not always, unconsciously provide an answer. Moments such as these are ordinary but invaluable. They help the analysand to discover his or her own unconscious work in a simple and explicit way, and they help the analyst develop his or her own relationship to that analysand's particular form of question and answer. Together, both participants enter the realm of questions from the unconscious.

8

'Caroline'

Caroline, who is thirty, grew up in London. She is a research scientist in psychopharmacology, which is also the field of her boyfriend, Edward. She has had casual relationships in the past, but Edward is her first serious boyfriend and they have been together for two years.

She is in her fourth year of four-times-weekly psycho-analysis. Although she talks about ending her treatment, it is clear to both the analyst and herself that further work needs to be done.

Caroline had an unremarkable childhood. She has a younger sister, also a scientist, and they have a civil relationship but they are not close; they were quite competitive as children. Her mother was a stay-at-home mum who was caring and fastidious but not very warm. The mother was on the silent side, devoted to the house, its chores, her husband and the family. Caroline's father was a general practitioner who was well liked by his patients. The daughters admired him and competed for his attention. He was supportive of them but, like his wife, he was not demonstratively affectionate.

Caroline is petite and wears business suits for work. She has wispy chestnut hair that often hangs over her face, so she is forever tidying her forehead. She is intelligent and intense, but humourless. She has a potential for liveli-ness which seems forestalled. It was for this reason, as well as difficulties in forming a relationship, that she sought analysis.

Finally, Caroline is a member of a yoga centre; not only does her analyst also attend, but the analyst serves on the centre's board of directors.

Session 1

Caroline:

I had a dream last night. I had invited several guests. But I hadn't prepared or bought anything, so there was nothing to drink or eat in the fridge. I went to my neighbour, Marge. She usually has a good collection of wine. I asked her whether she could help me. But she said she seemed not to have the wine after all and so she could not be of help.

The dream raises a question. 'Why have I invited guests to dinner and yet have not bought anything and have nothing to give them to drink or eat?'

I don't like to shop or prepare things for guests. At home usually I have nothing in the fridge. Yesterday Edward came home at ten o'clock in the evening and I couldn't offer him anything to eat. I was ashamed. But I hadn't thought that he might be hungry.

Her association that she does not like to shop or prepare anything is a statement, but it can be seen as a question: why not?

She free associates and Edward comes to mind. He came to dinner, but she had nothing to offer him to eat. Along a line of emotional thinking, she says she felt ashamed.

The analyst reported feeling the ring of the phrase 'I hadn't thought' to be a telling communication. We might add: what is the link to thinking?

He, unlike me, always has something in the fridge. He is a great cook and sometimes prepares wonderful meals for me.

She contrasts herself to Edward, who always has something in the fridge.

He is also a very good guide. When we hike in the Fens he is always well orientated. He looks at the map and then knows where we have to take our route. It's not worth it for me to try to do something like that by myself, so I leave it up to him and like to be guided by him.

This is a *radical free association*. Edward is also a guide; he is well orientated. Radical associations are noteworthy because of their *sharp* contrast with the previous association. Such juxtapositions strike the analyst's ear in a particular way, evoking increased pattern perception in the analyst's unconscious.

Caroline now provides an unconscious reason for why she does not have food and why she does not prepare. She likes to be looked after and guided by the other.

Analyst:
In your dream Marge hasn't said anything helpful for you . . .

The analyst's associations take her back to Marge's failure to be helpful. The analyst was surprised later that her comment seemed to avoid the material about Edward and returned the patient to the dream. Why?

Caroline:
Marge is from Scotland. She is the friend of a colleague from university. Both are painters. They spend a lot of time abroad. The two always complain about not having enough money. They feel disadvantaged in relation to people who earn more money than they do and blame them. They have an ideal utopia . . .

Another free association, following the line of logic about not having enough. (Not enough wine, not enough in the fridge, etc.) Question: 'Why do I not have enough?' Answer: 'Because I live elsewhere (abroad) in a utopia where I get all I need.'

The analyst, interestingly, has brought up Marge, and Caroline then free associates through Marge: her life, her habits and so forth. Together they pick an object, Marge, through whom to think projectively. This is the imaginary order of articulation.

Marge (Caroline's projective proxy) and Caroline's colleague from university live in the world of utopian dreams and therefore, says Caroline's unconscious, they feel disadvantaged vis-à-vis people who live in the *real world.*

Marge is on one side very lively and enjoys life, but on the other very frustrated, because she claims she is not getting enough recognition, which she would have deserved.

Here we observe a *binary associative link*: a lively Marge, but also a frustrated Marge, because she does not get recognition. Binary associations are links between two contiguous associations that carry splits in the ego or the object. They follow divided lines of thought whose meaning resides, in part, in this division. Why does the issue of recognition arise in the session? A radical juxtaposition, like a radical free association, speaks to the analyst's unconscious which, of course, also works according to such forms of logic.

Oh yes . . . recognition . . . I had a clash with the secretary of the psychopharmacology institute, where Edward works as an assistant. I wanted to go to a small congress they organise. I had missed the date for subscription. The secretary told me that there were already 120 participants instead of 90, which were planned. It would be impossible to get admission for me. I said that I'm Edward's partner – but she said this wouldn't matter, and that I should stop being so pushy.

The word 'recognition' is immediately repeated and it now leads the patient to other associations. Freud says that repetition is emphasis, so 'recognition' – or lack of it – may be an issue in the analysand's line of thought. We might ask: what does her preference for being fed by an other have to do with her feeling that she does not get enough recognition? And is she here opening up a line of thought to do with the issue of being seen, of whether her identity is observed?

The word 'recognition' also reminds the patient of an injury: she believes she should have been admitted for free – without having to do or prepare anything for herself – because of her relation to Edward. This kind of association provides the analyst with more unconscious material. Is Caroline saying that her dependence on Edward should license her to have a free meal ticket to anything in life? She is reminded of a provocative moment, but recalling this is also something of a challenging memory in the session. Such surprising comments are of high psychic value because they inevitably strike the analyst as perplexing. This is a moment when the patient's material is like a riddle. What does it mean that I go mad when a woman bars my way to invoking my free access sponsored by Edward?

When Edward came home, he told me that she went to him and warned him. She said that I was trying to take advantage of Edward's position and that this was

Another line of thought is opened, through a question: 'Who does this woman think I am?'

This seems Oedipally challenging, but it may also at the

an exploitation of our relationship. She told him to stop me. I went completely mad when I heard this. Who does this woman think I am? I was incensed . . . If someone like her puts a limit in front of me it enrages me. That she says I complained is impossible – and that she calls Edward.

same time follow another line of thought raised through the previous question, having to do with recognition. 'Who does this woman think I am?' could now also be understood as 'Whomever she *thinks* I am must *be* who I am.'

Caroline observes that if someone puts a limit in front of her it is enraging. Yet her unrealistic demand elicited a limit. Why is she asking for such a limit?

In the dream I already switched the points wrongly – I invited without having prepared anything.

The association to the dream seems inexplicable. What does this have to *No* do with what she has just said? Such manifest un-connection announces that the links are deeply unconscious. This is another radical free association.

> ! She's going back
> to 1st statement
> of the hour !

Perhaps you have noticed the curious wording in the previous association: 'Who does this woman think I am?' Does she not mean to say: 'Who does this woman think *she* is?' Why would Caroline switch positions between self and other? Is this what is meant by 'switching points'? This may be a line of thinking that expresses itself in the *syntactical order*, part of the *linguistic category*.

Analyst:
You don't want to need to do something like that.

The analyst does not know why she said this to the patient; it just arrived. But note the odd syntax.

Caroline:
And I *didn't want* to pay for the congress – it was even the most expensive price because I was too late. I wanted to ask the university where I work whether they would pay for me. Honestly, *they* should invite *me* to the congress without letting me pay! They should invite me as a *guest of honour*!

The patient moves from narrating differing lines of thought to enacting the self that seemed so entitled. It is as if she moves order, from *narrative* to *dramatic*, thus linking the emotions to the ideas presented.

In the dream, when it was badly threaded it doesn't work any more. I can't help myself, not even with Marge.

As before, the patient returns to the dream. It is puzzling. The syntactical breakdown (she leaves out the verb 'is') may be a formal change of order, from expressing herself coherently in language towards moving into a dream-image logic.

Analyst:
The question is, why is it badly threaded? Why did you invite your guests without having prepared anything? Perhaps preparing something would mean not being a guest of honour, just a normal person.

The analyst, however, seems to know what the patient means by 'badly threaded'. Is she asking why the dream is badly threaded so that she cannot make sense of it? If so, is this why she returns to the dream, as if by re-thinking she can rethread it? Is she drawing attention to the need for further threads of thought to be discovered before she can answer the questions posed?

Caroline:
I hoped, *somehow*, that there would be a good solution, without me *doing anything*. I was *sure* that the Dean of Studies would be *very pleased* when he saw me. The secretary should have made it possible that I could participate, even if I didn't subscribe on time. I'm really very upset about having to pay £90. I am absolutely sure that I want to participate. It's only because of this *damn* secretary that I cannot be admitted.

The patient associates to the Dean of Studies, but the puzzling and childlike form of her narrative introduces another category and line of logic. She continues to dramatise her plight. Her actions answer her question, 'Why am I not admitted?' Her behaviour states: 'Because you are not grown up enough to attend something like this.' The *relational category* joins the *linguistic category* as both forms of thinking converge to emphasise her conflict.

By the way, at the Yoga Centre I didn't pay either . . .

Caroline seems to be provoking the analyst by pointing out that she is admitted free to the Yoga Centre. The analyst says that the patient must feel this is through her, the analyst.

Analyst:
You think your special admission there works through me . . .

So how do we reconcile these two female others: one who bars her, the other who gets her in for free? Caroline juxtaposes two figures: the analyst who lets her in free (no restrictions, pure pleasure) and the secretary who bars her. The analyst fulfils her dream and is the ideal other; the secretary is the reality principle that causes her (assisted by projectee-Marge) to complain about not getting things her way.

But the two figures exemplify the difference in these two talking worlds. Caroline can say anything that comes to mind to the analyst, but she cannot say whatever pops into her head in the outside world. Thus she is testing the difference between the maternal order – the sequestered world of mother and infant – and the paternal order – the social world that all of us are eventually expected to honour and work within.

Caroline:

Well, I think I don't have to pay like everybody else there. Perhaps it's a test: whether they would kick me out or not. I am pleased that Edward now must do something, to make it possible that I can take part at the congress.

When Caroline says that perhaps it is a test she now answers the question posed at the beginning of the session. She is testing out others, including Edward, to see where the limits reside. Testing which limits? The limits of acceptable behaviour if one is to take part in the congress of life.

Caroline's acting out may be a form of separation from the figure whom she has declared looks after her. She has forced a situation where this is no longer possible. Thus what looks like an infantile action may ironically also be a lurch towards more independent thinking and behaving.

Session 2

Caroline:
That was a strange session last time.

There is silence for two minutes.

Today I went first to your old address, to Kensington High Street.

The patient begins with a free association. She says that the last

I was so much involved in talking to you in my mind that I went to the old office. I'm so tired of all the dates, which determine my life. And I'm fed up with my work at the research centre.

session was strange, but she links this associatively to a parapraxis: she has just visited the analyst's old office. She associates such an action to an internal conversation with the analyst and then free associates to being tired of dates that determine her life and work. Thus in one short sequence she has made four links in the chain of ideas: (1) the last session was strange; (2) I went to your old office; (3) because I was talking to you; (4) I am tired of dates and determination.

How do we understand this sequential logic? I could put it into an interpretation: 'Yesterday you behaved strangely in the session and today, outside the session, you were lost in imaginary dialogue with me and went back to our beginning, and perhaps to the beginning of life, like a new-born who does not have to think of dates, obligations, and work in the real world.'

Well in the last session we talked about my admission to the congress and the parallel situation at the Yoga Centre. Afterwards I was astonished about the urge to have a special status. It reminds me of all the things which I couldn't bear about my friend Rina, who always wanted to be someone special. I thought, it is because of this need of being someone special that I'm still in analysis and have difficulties thinking of this ending.

Caroline has changed rhetorical and character form. No longer theatrical and childlike, she is a reflecting adult, who asks about her behaviour. She makes her own interpretation through free association: behaving in a childlike way asserts her need to be special, which means that she needs more analysis. She is anxious, perhaps, that the analyst perceive this, lest her otherwise important developments in the treatment be seen as reason to end the analysis . . . too soon.

Note that it is the word 'special' that carries the free-associative link. It calls up other special times.

Analyst:
So ending analysis for you means losing this special status?

Caroline:

Playing the piano was my special relation to my aunt. Giving up piano was like betraying my aunt. When I stop analysis here, my connection to you will break, which is a guarantee for something else. My relation to you contains something of my self.

Caroline associates from the transference line to her past: the relationship to her aunt. This is a radical free association and as such it raises the listener's interest. It is evidence of the analysand's intensity of unconscious work, as she brings in more material for thought. The patient then consciously links the aunt to the analyst, joining transference-thinking to the line of thought that we might call 'remembering my aunt'.

Analyst:

Because I listen to you . . .

The analyst links the material by association: listening to the piano, listening to speech.

Caroline:

Yes – but it is the guarantee for having access to something very important, which I can't have otherwise without you.

Caroline answers associatively. She adds that such listening is a guarantee for access to something which she could not have without this good maternal figure.

A silence of two minutes follows before Caroline continues.

I didn't choose you because of your status at the Psychoanalytical Society. I even didn't know about it when I chose you. I chose your name because I liked it. I went to another analyst who had her practice nearer to my flat. But I liked your address too: Kensington High Street. When I had seen you both, I knew that you and I would fit.

A new line of association opens up the session further. The question is: 'Why did I choose you?' Answer: Because of the analyst's name. Caroline associates to another name: that of the analyst's street, which contains the word 'high'. After she has seen the other analyst – closer in proximity to her – Caroline chooses this analyst because she has seen both and knows that she and this analyst would 'fit'. So although she denies that she chose the analyst because of the analyst's status in the Society, Caroline's associations seem to disagree with her conscious assertion, as the name of the analyst's street associates her with being up high – in other words, to her status. What is the relativity of the status? High in relation to what? To a rival analyst who, though closer to her in space, is not such a good fit? What might she be thinking?

In some way I find access to myself in your presence. And I don't find it when I'm alone.

Caroline associates from the choice of the analyst–object to being able to find herself when in the presence of the analyst: not alone. So the object choice seems to be preverbal – the sound of the name, the scene of the address, the sight of the analyst: these early phenomena allow her to be accessed. In this line the patient lets the analyst know that the choice is made at a very early infantile level. She is also telling the analyst that she cannot be alone, thus linking this moment back to being guided by Edward.

I found the same access to myself in the presence of my aunt. She contained something precious of me, as you do too.

She associates to feeling the same way in the presence of her aunt, but she is more specific. The special part of her was contained *within* the aunt.

We may now answer, in part, the question raised a moment ago about the name of the analyst and the name of the street. Caroline feels the same in the presence of the analyst and the aunt. The associations are to the infantile period. Thus the aunt is associated, as is the analyst, with the maternal figure. So in comparing the analyst who is close with the analyst who is afar, and choosing the latter, Caroline may be stating that the object of her love was not the mother (the one who was close) but the aunt (who was further away, but with whom Caroline felt a better fit). Her associations, however, ask another question: What kind of fit?

Analyst:
You mean, you were someone special for her, as you think to be for me.   Cold

Caroline:
Creativity and all sorts of self-expression were the most important things in life for my aunt. She was happy about every personal expression of mine, be it piano, telling stories or whatever. And in some way I experience the same here with you.

A silence of one minute follows before Caroline continues.

I had also the same name as my aunt had.

This fact seems fateful. What did the mother mean by naming Caroline after her sister? Was it the mother who destined her daughter to be closer to the aunt, and if so, why? Why should Caroline's identity derive from a sister rather than from the mother? We now know that in picking the analyst by name, Caroline does to the analyst what her mother did to her. We do not know the meaning of the analyst's name to Caroline – obviously that will arrive at some point in the analysis – but her unconscious follows a maternal logic. This is an expression, therefore, in the order of identification, a part of the relational category of expression.

She thought a lot about deep themes, about life and great literature. I felt life as uncanny but also thrilling, and I liked to discuss deep questions with my aunt.

Caroline is engaged in a kind of remembering of her aunt, following an emotional line of thought opened in the previous session. But the uncanny (around being named) continues and is now associated with being thrilled to discuss deep questions, something also taking place in Caroline's relationship to her analyst.

I experienced her as very young and mobile – she discussed with me the questions which one has in adolescence. I had chosen my aunt as my highest ideal.

She recollects the questions one has as an adolescent and thus specifies the area she presents to her analyst for understanding: the adolescent self.

At her side I disappeared. I didn't see myself any more, because she was in the centre of my attention. There is always this conviction in me that I wouldn't be able to develop something inside of me, that I wouldn't be able to live something for which I have the potential.

This is a *vivid free association*. Caroline provides a startling insight that she disappeared inside her aunt; she lost sight of herself. This is evidence of unconscious work and unconscious insight. The analysand, by herself, is realising that if you idealise the object, your own self can become lost inside the ideal object, a problem common to adolescent psychology. Caroline's comment is a deeply moving realisation of the loss of contact with her true self, which cannot live because it has been projected into the aunt.

The radical free association also partly answers the question implicit in her associations, when we asked 'What kind of fit?' It is a fitting of the self in relation to an ideal other: to the other on high. So Caroline's choice of analyst was based on an idealisation.

Let us imagine an interpretation: 'After thinking of how part of you is inside me and about why you fear loss of connection, interestingly, you then seem to answer why you must leave such a valued relationship, because, as you say, it robs you of your own identity as you get lost inside the ideal other: aunt or myself.'

This interpretation would not be sufficient in itself because the analysand has raised the issue of feeling that she has lost her potential. This might be the time to link up the analysand's logic of sequence over these two sessions. Thus one might add the following: 'You have wondered why it is that you are unable to prepare for things, to have something inside you to feed the other. Why this loss of potential? But I think today and yesterday you have answered why this is so: that by getting Edward and others to guide

you, like your aunt, you foreclose
your own development. It is so
interesting, isn't it, that you know
this unconsciously.'

Analyst:
Your aunt and I have to help you
with this.

Caroline:
Yes, but analysis is precisely this –
don't you think so?

Analyst:
Analysis is also what you will take
with you when you leave me.

*A silence of five minutes follows
before the analyst continues.*

You're silent.

Caroline:
Me alone and my unconscious –
this is not enough. It needs two.
Otherwise my unconscious becomes
dominant. My fate, that I don't
bring out something which is
sticking inside me . . . above all
when I'm alone, I won't get it out . . .

This is a *profound realisation* in the
analysand's unconscious thinking: a
profound realisation in consciousness
of something known but not yet
thought. Such realisations arrive out
of free association and are received
by the analysand as if they are gifts
from the unconscious.

Note the radical free association
that follows: of something 'sticking
inside me . . . above all when I'm
alone'. What is one to make of this?
As always, one must wait to see what
the patient talks about next, as only
the logic of sequence can inform the
analyst of the meaning of such a
startling image.

Yesterday I took a mirror of my
aunt's. It belonged to my sister. I
robbed this mirror from my sister's
flat and took it to my place. I felt so
guilty about robbing again. And
about being so materialistic.

Caroline's next associations proceed
from the striking disclosure above to
the confession that she has stolen her
aunt's mirror from her sister.

What does the sequential logic
tell us? Surely it must be that she
would like to bring out what is
sticking inside her – above all when

she is alone – and that what she must get out (in the analysis) is something that had been inside the sister, but that is now inside Caroline. She gained it by stealth. So if you steal something that should thus be kept secret, how do you now bring it out and make use of it? Perhaps you tell the analyst. Perhaps it has to be brought out through speech.

What can this mean? This certainly adds to the complexity of the logic of these associations. Let us see if we can make sense of the sequence. I will put it into an interpretation: 'You feel there is something true of you that is inside but cannot get out to be free, but perhaps it is incarcerated in you because you feel you have stolen it: it is not really yours, but someone else's. How could you steal your own identity? Why would it be in the other to begin with and not in yourself? By stealing your aunt's mirror, held by your sister, don't you think that maybe, as the last image in the aunt's mirror was of your sister, that you felt your aunt – who had *your* name, not your sister's name – should mirror you and you mirror her? By retrieving the mirror, do you not think you were getting back your image and also your name, which is linked to your image?'

Analyst:
Robbing must have something to do with not being able to get out what is inside you. Perhaps you can let it out here because you are sure that I won't be critical of you.

The analyst is unconsciously in touch with the sequence of ideas. It is the end of the hour but she feels a need to make some links in the associative material. She reassures Caroline that her theft – easy prey for criticism – is meaningful and that it has to do with her need to get something articulated.

Discussion

Before discussing the sequential logic over these two sessions, let us have a look at a few of the free associations, in order to better understand the simplicity – and yet the accuracy – of associative representation.

Caroline is thinking unconsciously about why she does not prepare food for her guests. Edward comes to mind. She says he is a wonderful cook and then says he is also a very good guide – so we can see that cooking and guiding (or looking after) are linked. What is the logic of these two otherwise separate ideas? Instead of wishing to cook for (and guide) her others, Caroline states that she wishes to be cooked for and therefore led.

When they are linked by Freud's theory of logic, we can see that these two simple statements become incredibly informative.

Indeed, on the basis of this one association Caroline is consciously able to state that it is not worth guiding herself as she can leave it up to Edward to do it for her. She has not said that this is why she does not bother to prepare meals or cook for others, but she has made the link to being looked after – a free-associative connection that, as I shall discuss in a moment, reflects the work of unconscious insight.

Sometimes free associations occur *between* analyst and analysand. We can see this following Caroline's statement that she likes to be guided by Edward. The analyst, much to her surprise on reflection, takes the lead and asks Caroline to return to the dream: 'In your dream,' the analyst pointed out, 'Marge hasn't said anything helpful.' It seems puzzling that the analyst returns to the issue of Marge – in fact, it is as though the analyst is prompted by Caroline's observation that she likes to be led. However, in guiding Caroline back to the dream, the analyst also guides her to another form of thinking: the projective. It may be that the analyst senses unconsciously that the narrative line of logic has momentarily reached its conclusion, and by shifting order (from the narrative line to the projective), she seeks to open up a different form of thinking and expression of the unconscious ideas. It seems to be a good choice on the analyst's part because it releases a considerable amount of free associating.

We note, therefore, that while in general an interpretation will connect the lines of thought as they have been delivered in the patient's oral discourse, sometimes an analyst's passing comment can be as manifestly odd as the analysand's. In the example here the reason for this change of form is in fact most astute, but one would never have made this as a conscious decision. It is spontaneous, not premeditated, and part of the psychoanalyst's unconscious perception of Caroline's thought process.

Let us review the sequential logic over Caroline's two sessions. She begins with a dream in which she does not have enough food prepared for her guests. Her associations take her to Edward, who both has enough food prepared and is also a good guide. She concludes that it is not worth it for her to guide herself if she has someone like Edward to do it for her. Caroline's free associations answer the dream question, 'Why have anything prepared if someone will look after you?' In the second session, however, she looks back on both the content and the childlike behaviour of the first session and she associates to an aunt whom she idealised as a child and upon whom she was very dependent. The aunt made her feel very special – indeed, Caroline felt she had access to herself through the aunt, just as she does in the presence of her analyst. Then, in a startling association, Caroline says that at her aunt's side she felt she disappeared. She reports stealing her aunt's mirror from her sister. These free-flowing associations indicate a high degree of unconscious thinking as Caroline struggles to answer the question of the first session: 'Why do I not prepare anything and just give in to the other, to be guided?' She replies that in the course of idealising the other (Edward, her aunt, the analyst), although she is looked after and feels special, she has lost her true self through an act of merger. She cannot see herself with her mind's eye in an internal mirror. The solution? By robbing her sister of the mirror (an early primitive act in the evolution towards self-establishment), she is taking the idealising mirror

idealizing is bad!

back. Caroline will be able to see herself now without being beside the aunt. I think the associations suggest that she will eventually be able to imagine, sense and believe in herself as an independent agent, once she can divorce herself from these idealising relationships.

Now let's look at another line of associations:

> Me alone and my unconscious . . . It needs two. Otherwise my unconscious becomes dominant. My fate, that I don't bring out something . . . sticking inside me . . . above all when I'm alone, I won't get it out.

From here Caroline associates to stealing her aunt's mirror from her sister. How do we understand this line of thought? She states that she cannot live alone and *therefore* must live in the presence of another. Why? Because, she says, her unconscious would otherwise become too dominant. In what way? What is it about her unconscious that would dominate her? Let's see what she says immediately following this. She says her fate is that she does not bring out something that sticks inside her, above all when she is alone. That surely is puzzling, isn't it? It is a form of condensation – and our task is to see if we can unpack the overdetermination of this associative content. The clue, I think, resides in the word 'sticking'. Caroline's syntax is confusing, as she seems to be saying that the reason her unconscious is dominant is that she doesn't bring out something, a something that is sticking inside her. We have to build on the grammar of the sentence to discover the logic of the statement. I think she is saying, unconsciously, that she cannot be alone because she would be dominated by an adhesive quality inside her which she dare not bring out (while alone) because it would overwhelm her with her own neediness (her stickiness, her adhesiveness). When she is in the presence of the other, such neediness is bearable, as we have seen with her aunt, with Edward, and with the analyst. We recognise in this line of thought the following statement:

> I cannot be alone because my needs demand a mother who will never come and this need then overwhelms me;

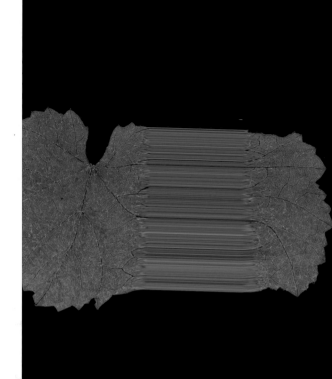

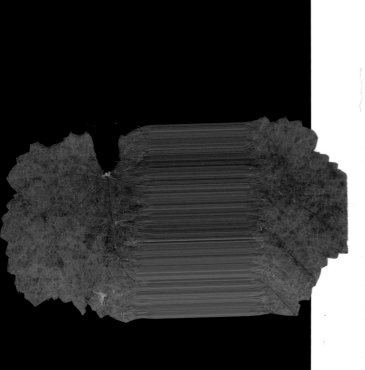

but if I am in the presence of the other then I am not so overwhelmed. Unfortunately, however, my use of the other to satisfy this need means that I have never allowed my idiom of need – my true self – to emerge in any relationship.

It is important to pay attention to Caroline's syntactical line of expression. We can see that her syntax is confusing because it is a syntactical speech act. She is talking about a fear of merging with the other, but her speech breaks down into a *con-fusion*. The loss of syntactical integrity (or maturity of speech) happens at the moment when Caroline is thinking about the infantile part of her personality.

Although Caroline's psychoanalyst has been crucial to the path of her associations, at no point has the analyst made the connections discussed above. But all of them have been latently stated in the implicit logic of Caroline's leaps from one manifest content to another. The logic lies in the unconscious reasoning resident in such leaps.

Caroline's session helps us to see how a patient can pose a question and proceed to use the hour to raise answers and further questions. This interrogative imperative is apparent throughout Caroline's two sessions, which also illustrate a high degree of complexity. In particular they help us consider both radical free associations and vivid juxtapositions. When analysands free associate it is not uncommon for the manifest contents to seem so disconnected as to be startling. Instead of this being a form of random thinking – which is the way psychiatry often views free associations – such looseness of thought is actually the space in which mental freedom opens up to articulate ongoing unconscious ideation.

Analysts accustomed to working with free associations have come to regard such radical or vivid moments as illuminating. The non-sequitur nature of these associations inspires the analyst's unconscious to think along very odd lines which, precisely because they are so idiomatic, more often than not yield deep insight into the self.

Rather than returning to the ground covered in the commentary, let us instead look at Caroline's dream in the first session. We recall that she asks Marge if she has any wine, because Marge has a good wine collection. But she doesn't have any, so Caroline cannot borrow any. When she returns to the subject of Marge – having discussed in the meantime how Edward is a good guide – she tells of Marge complaining about money and Marge's feeling that she is disadvantaged in relation to other people.

As we discussed in the case of Arlene, when listening to an analysand's utterances it is essential for the psychoanalyst to be open to the phonemic chain of meaning: to the sound of words. Other words may exist phonemically within the employed word, or there may be signifiers that point to other signifiers in a chain of meaning. Analysts need to allow themselves to hear these other words. It does not require deliberative concentration in the here and now; it only necessitates, through training, the abandonment of a kind of hearing block.

So let us return to Caroline's dream. Marge has a good wine collection. Listen to the word 'wine'. What other word does it sound like? We can hear, I think, the word 'whine'. (Indeed, the play on this particular signifier forms the basis of a well-known joke: 'What's my wife's favourite wine? "When do I get to go to Bali?"!')

Marge's large collection of wine, then, can be understood as Marge having a large collection of 'whine'. After associating to Edward's generous provision of food and direction, Caroline returns to Marge and her complaints about not having enough money. Caroline projects the whining part of her personality into Marge and, through talking about her, sustains the discourse of the complaining self. But what would it mean 'to run out of whine', especially for an experienced collector of whinges? Marge (the projectee) has run out of the wine to be borrowed by Caroline in order to serve it up to Edward. So might it be that this is the sort of food best run out of and not served up? Perhaps. Interestingly, Caroline pursues this line of thought by complaining about the expense of the psychopharmacology conference – like Marge, she complains about money – and Edward is brought into the field of complaint.

The next session, however, begins with Caroline surprised by her own impetuous behaviour in the previous hour. This gives further credibility to the idea that one line of thought is expressing the wish to stop whingeing. If so, then her dream, her projectee, and her silly argument with the institute's secretary would constitute unconscious irony. It would be a way for Caroline to objectify and poke fun at an infantile part of herself.

The ironic position is a double occupation: one position is opposed by another. Caroline says she wants to be looked after but the way she behaves mocks this statement. Further, by splitting the self into not just two positions, but two different orders of representation (narrative and dramatic), Caroline objectifies the part of her which the ironic position targets. By acting childlike she gets it out, in full view, and upon reflection is able to wonder about it. Thus what might appear at first to be an enactment aimed at gaining something from the analyst within the transference is in fact a form of self-analysis, using the analyst as a type of mirror to reflect the self-in-action. To be theatrical requires an audience, and Caroline needs the analyst to bear witness to the performance. To this extent an enactment is a *use* of the object (to objectify the self through the other) rather than a *relationship* to the object. It is aimed not at eliciting a response from the other – apart from the audient's indication that he or she is a witness – but at using the other through whom to act out (that is, to realise) a part of the self that can be visible only through this means of expression.

The above constitutes a complex line of free-associative thought.

We have considered two sessions in the life of an analysand and we can see how complex just two analytic hours can be. From what we have seen we can know only a fraction of Caroline's thinking, but what we learn we discover by following her lines of thought and the categories and orders in which she thinks them.

As we turn now to the case of Annie, and three sessions in a row, we will see even more clearly how immensely complex unconscious articulation can become in psychoanalysis.

9

'Annie'

At the time of these sessions Annie was thirty-five. She was born and brought up in Scotland and began analysis in her late twenties. Trained as a cinematographer, she has worked on several feature films but her passion is documentaries. She developed an interest in making films that peeped through the windows of homes at night, illuminating – in an Edward Hopper-like manner – the lives of ordinary people.

Her mother was a passionate Labour Party activist who lectured widely across Scotland and the whole of the UK. Annie's father was a minister of the church with an interest in logical positivist philosophy. Annie was raised by her maternal grandmother, who lived in the home and to whom she felt quite close – in contrast to her mother, whose way of holding her she found 'uncomfortable'. Annie's grandmother had special fears of bacterial infections and part of her routine was to impose rigorous toilet training and anal hygiene: she would give Annie suppositories each day in order to purge her, and would scrub her anus with a warm soapy cloth. Annie recalls having her first orgasm during the administration of one of these bathings. Her maternal aunt, who lived down the street, would often visit and read her stories. She recalls that the aunt loved to read her the story of Pandora.

Annie's parents divorced when she was eleven. Her father remarried and his new wife soon gave birth to a stillborn son. Annie did not like her stepmother, but she was nonetheless deeply affected by this death.

Annie came to analysis because she had been unable to maintain stable relationships with men. She had recently broken up with James, a landscape architect, with whom she had been in a relationship for about a year. At the time of the sessions reported below, she had just met a new man, Marcus, and was passionate about him but afraid that the relationship would not succeed.

Marcus is a chartered accountant who works in a large bank. His wife died of foot cancer some two years before these sessions.

Carlos, who is also in analysis, is a very good friend of Annie's. He is a schoolteacher but as a hobby he works as a clown for private functions, and occasionally in the theatre.

Tess is a student on a placement, working with Annie.

Annie is deeply fond of her analyst. She is working through a period of passionate yet restrained positive trans-ference (transference neurosis), which took up much of the first years of their work.

She is a beautiful woman, over six feet tall, with blonde hair down to her waist and bright blue eyes. Although she buys 'off the peg', she wears subtly coordinated clothing that reflects her artistic taste. She never arrives in the same outfit twice and she expresses her moods through her choice of colours and style. She can look like a neo-hippy one day, a 1970s Antonioni figure the next, and a farm girl the day after.

Annie is very talkative and dramatic. At the beginning of the analysis she would talk non-stop, leaving the analyst with little space to speak. Her demonstrative style and acute questions often had him off-guard and he found it rather difficult to think. Nonetheless he found her likeable and could see that she was dedicated to her analysis and hard at work.

For the purpose of understanding these sessions it is important to bear in mind that Annie often speaks in rapid-fire bursts, accenting the positive, putting many things together in a compressed way. On the other hand, she can suddenly change her mood and be quiet and reflective.

On the Wednesday, the day of the third reported session, she was due to have a cyst removed from the lower part of her back.

A few further details are relevant. As a child, Annie would stand in front of a reflective window that mirrored her. She would try to see whether the image moved even if she did not – she was certain that it did. She was very shy as a child and daydreamed a lot, to the point where teachers were critical of her for not paying attention in class. In her pre-adolescence Annie was admonished for 'sexually inappropriate' play with other children. This seems to have consisted simply of rubbing up against other children now and then, but it has left her feeling that she did something quite wrong – of a sexual nature – when she was a child; she feels that she harmed the other children.

In the week before these three sessions she dreamt of being 'a larva on the verge of metamorphosis'.

Session 1 (Monday)

Annie:
The weather was so beautiful over the weekend. I spent a lot of time in the garden. I emailed Marcus about how I went and bought a marigold plant and how I felt like I was setting it free. I freed it from the little pot it was in.

For the next minute or two she describes in fine detail everything she did to prepare it for planting.

It was fun and muddy.

Analyst:
And a nice metaphor . . .

Annie:
Mmm. I bought it because it had a bloom. I've been wanting to tell you how good you look lately. Like life must be agreeing with you in some way. It seems you've changed a fair amount since we started this analysis. Last autumn you seemed

This Monday session is an account of Annie's weekend, when she is thinking with her friend Carlos about her new relation to Marcus. A subplot is her planting. She wants the analyst to know that she feels freer than she has in the past, that she appreciates the analysis, and she conveys the impression that she enjoys being in the session.

Annie's next association is to buying the marigold because it had a 'bloom', and this springs a free association to her analyst, that she had been wanting to tell him that he looked good.

She says that *he has changed* 'a fair amount' since the analysis started to get bogged down a bit, but whatever that was, it's gone. Your colour is good.

and refers back to the autumn when she says he seemed to get *bogged* down a bit. Then, intriguingly, she says 'whatever *that was*, it's gone' and she proclaims that his 'colour is good'.

The logic of narrative sequence seems to be as follows: I have purchased a plant in a pot and set it free. In the analysis I have set you free.

The chain of ideas – buying, setting free from pot (we may think of toilet), fun in the mud, and her reference to the analyst being bogged down ('bog' can be a reference both to the toilet and to mud) – may well be a line of thought serving both an anal drive *and* the grandmother's anal ministrations – that is: 'I must free the shit that is inside me and find a way to make it fun and blooming. To do so, however, is contingent on freeing the shit in the other who is bogged down in it.'

A potted plant is an object of which the lower part is dirt and roots, the middle section is green stem and the top has blossoms on. It may be symbolic of Annie's body. In liberating it from the pot by putting it into the earth, the lower part is allowed a wider contact with the anal environment. The statements 'whatever that was, it's gone' and 'your colour is good' might refer to the analyst's faecal evacuation of the bog-issue that has been eliminated, now giving him a good colour.

But we still need to wonder further: from what else might she have freed the analyst? The patient implicitly raises this question when she says 'but whatever that was, it's gone'. What is gone?

Analyst:

You seem more free to say that now.

The analyst implicitly recognises that however true Annie's observation, she is also talking about herself.

Annie:

Yes, though I'm not saying directly that I'm interested in you and the 'I wish . . .' sorts of things. It's more 'I appreciate.' I got asked for my driving licence yesterday and told the policeman, 'Oh, you're handing out random acts of kindness, are you?' Once that happened when I was travelling and I wouldn't give my ID to the guy. I was being playful and said to him, 'You just want to know something about me.'

Her next association is to being asked for her licence, and she transforms a kind of interrogation of her into a joke. Her jolly tone follows her analyst's comment that she now seems more free. She enacts what she is talking about.

The phrase 'I wouldn't give my ID to the guy' has multiple meanings. By joking with the other she deters him from really gaining access to her identity, while unconsciously saying, within the transference, that she will not hand over her identity to the analyst.

Well, I had a real reaction to Marcus's attention to me, as you saw on Friday. It was old stuff, and threw me back, which I didn't like. I was talking about it with Carlos, who had an intense reaction to my reaction, to my feeling lesser than Marcus in some way, Marcus being such an accomplished person. He seems to have his head on straight. He's a success. Then Carlos asked me if I think of him as successful. I told him, 'You seem to think you're not – you seem not happy with what you have.' So he took that overnight as 'I think of him as a non-success.' He emailed the next morning, saying he couldn't live with having a friend who thought of him this way. He lashed out at me for who I put on pedestals. Some of it hit home.

Annie now narrates the story of Carlos's reaction to her account of her relationship with Marcus. Annie has discovered from her analysis that she subordinates herself to men, something that Carlos points out to her. She passes into Carlos her objection to such subordination.

She free associates now through projective identification, as Carlos is the one to carry the pain. His feelings carry and elaborate her own.

She praises Marcus in Carlos's presence, inducing a feeling in Carlos that he is a lesser man than Marcus. In so doing, she brings about in Carlos her own feelings of being diminished through idealisation of the other.

Carlos's reaction indicates the *affective power* of her associations, as Carlos is disturbed for days. He now enacts Annie's objection to the idealised figure. This now 'hits home', so insight follows projective identification.

In some ways he was right, that putting Marcus on a pedestal will make it hard for me to relate to him. I cried for a while thinking about it. I emailed back. He called me later, still smarting that I said he was stupid. I said to him, 'You're not fighting against me but somebody else – you're pinning things on me I don't feel. What's this about? Your mother?' He just let loose and said, 'Oh, God, I just remembered something I haven't thought about in years.' Long story short, he remembered his mum had called him 'stupid' frequently, and now he was connecting this to his issue of thinking he's not bright. Apparently, his mother couldn't recognise any intelligence in him. I told him: '*Please* take this to your analyst!' He said he would if he could remember to.

He came over later and helped me with my studio. It needed to be braced. We worked on it together and he was trying to figure out the angles of the wood he was cutting. He used a protractor. I had an idea and said, 'Would this work?', but it didn't. Then I had another idea that did work. I'm watching him at this point and not wanting to correct him; I felt like I was figuring it out but should let him figure it out for himself, which he did. Spatially, he does have limits on how he thinks and I think very well spatially. I didn't want to let him know. Then at dinner he said, 'You're really good at solving spatial problems.' I said, 'Well, I'm a film-maker.' Anyway, I do have a tendency to put people up on pedestals, so with that thought I emailed Marcus back as an

Annie's own affect catches up with her, now that it is no longer lodged in Carlos.

Annie's rather glib retort to Carlos passes the issue back to the mother as the origin of the state of feeling diminished.

'He just let loose' may continue the anal line of thought: something coming out that has to do with the mother-line.

In Annie's 'weekend analysis' of Carlos she seems to be compensating for the loss of the analyst through identification with him. But '*Please* take this to your analyst!' is also a self-directive which she is presently enacting. Here the narrative and transferential orders of free association converge. The word 'please' is emphatic, so we add the sonic category as part of the logic of associations.

She free associates to Carlos helping her with her studio and the main line of thought here is that she had many ideas about what he could do but she thought it better to let him 'figure it out for himself'. Thus the transference line of expression continues in that she is acting as if she were the analyst with an analysand, allowing him to figure things out for himself. Freud stated that repetition is emphasis, and a word grabs our attention: 'figure'. It is first introduced in 'he was trying to figure out the angles', then she says, 'I felt like I was figuring it out but should let him figure it out'. This word is repeated seven more times in the hour. (Importantly, the analyst repeats the word later when he says, 'It *is* a good feeling to figure something out.') 'Figure' is a word with many meanings. It does mean to think things through, but it is also a ordinary person, in grief from a terrible loss. Now, he wants to get together.

It was painful with Carlos. Both our issues hit in the same spot so it took a while to figure out.

signifier for the self's body, usually that of a woman. So 'to figure' may mean, in the context of this session, to think things out both through the body and about the body.

One thing to figure out is something of a riddle. The patient talks about how 'painful with Carlos' the weekend was, adding, 'Both our issues hit in the same spot so it took a while to figure out.' We know that, manifestly, the pain with Carlos over the weekend was over Carlos's feeling that Annie had put him down. Annie made reparation by allowing Carlos to help her with her studio – to 'brace it' and their friendship – by not telling him what to do.

She thus seems to have found a solution to the Carlos problem. But what exactly has she figured out? She has decided that the solution to diminishment of him is to encourage his own creativity, not to dominate him.

I figured it out while I was shopping for marigolds. I still want to find somebody like you.

But what might be meant by this overdetermination of lines of thought? Annie links figuring things out, with buying a plant, with *finding* someone like her analyst.

I really don't think I'm putting you on a pedestal, but I don't know how you are in life outside here. Yet I do know how you are in here. I don't think I would have figured out what I did without what we've gone through in here guided by you. A relationship outside here would have more equality maybe . . . It seems to have gone in both directions here. The feeling is I'd like to try it in the other way.

Her love of her analyst lingers, obviously. But she is aware of her love of him and finds that their relationship in the session – though not what she would like at best – is still special. Annie very directly refers to the help she has received from her analyst and to its equality of sorts.

Analyst:
It *is* a good feeling to figure something out.

Annie:
It kind of illuminates the
difficulties I had with James. That
didn't happen enough. If this had
been James and I was bumping up,
he'd have said, 'This is what I have
to have – you *must not* think of me
as unsuccessful.' Carlos listened,
heard something and figured it out.
And I figured something out too.
Maybe I'm willing to accept more
responsibility. That was hard to do
with James because he wouldn't
accept any. So I had to take a
defensive posture.

I had a dream on Saturday night.
At work, in real life, Ines has had a
rough pregnancy and ended up
having a caesarean. In my dream, I
was with her. Oh, the first thing
she said was, 'I have a fever – I
don't feel well.' I knew she was
going into labour. I asked the
doctor if that was normal. He said
'yes'. So the delivery started. I
could feel her intense strong pain,
then it was normal, then again I
could feel the intensity. Instead of a
caesarean, she actually gave birth.

It seems straightforward. There's
the marigold, the birth. The pain
about Marcus and Carlos was like a
birthing pain. Essential. *(pauses)* I
was disturbed by something you
said at the end on Friday. It felt
like I sometimes feel when
teaching, as if I'm having a hard
time getting into the depths and
doing the figuring, and it was like

Implicit in this comparison of two
people taking responsibility for
working something through is
recognition that her analyst does
take responsibility for the evocative
impact of the positive transference.

The dream continues many lines of
thought but one now becomes more
prominent in the session: the concept
of freeing something. In real life Ines
had a caesarean section, but not in
the dream. In the dream Annie is
with Ines and shares her pain, and
therefore she can endure the pain
even though she is not feeling well.
Like many dreams, this is a riddle,
here involving the associative line:
plant out of pot, analyst out of bog,
baby out of the body of the mother.
We know the patient's history and as
such it may cross our minds that her
grandmother gave her anal
suppositories. This is the anal
equivalent of a caesarean section,
where the contents are removed by
semi-surgical intervention and the
self is not allowed a natural birth.

This is followed by facile free
associations: 'It seems
straightforward. There's the
marigold, the birth.' This is a speech
act that is glib, a throw-away.
    Even though she stresses that the
affect – the pain of Marcus and
Carlos that she likens to birthing pain
– is 'essential', she pauses and then
says she is disturbed by a comment

you were saying I was struggling with something that had already been figured out and so I was sliding backwards. You weren't helping me. You were frustrated with me, like, 'Hasn't she got that yet?'

made by the analyst in a previous session, that she is having a hard time 'getting into the depths and doing the figuring'. Why does this thought arise now? It follows a shallow set of associations and triggers another line of thought within the patient that indicates that she knows she is avoiding the depths of the matter.

This is an important moment. The patient has made a facile statement and her affect accompanies it. What is most interesting is the patient's demonstration that she knows this! Indeed, the insight follows her sonic stress, 'Essential', followed by a pause. In this pause, this reflective moment, the memory of something the analyst said on Friday arises. This is a good example of unconscious work; she is thinking through her resistances and defences.

I did something this morning. I read James's email. Right away I saw a message from the woman I think he picked up with right away after I moved out. She said in this poetic way, 'Let's each make love with whomever and watch and grade the lover.' That's a really interesting concept! What is James thinking and feeling? To do that, he would have to let go of some of that rigidity he has. It piques my interest what he would do with such an offer. So I want to know, has anyone ever offered that to you?

We then get a radical free association: clicking on the email. As if in answer to the question posed above – 'what depths am I ignoring?' – Annie moves straight to her voyeuristic interest in the other's sexual fantasy life.

We will return to her interesting statement 'What is James thinking and feeling?' but for now let us concentrate on her question to the analyst ('has anyone ever offered that to you?'), which is invasive. The move from invasion of James's privacy to invasion of the analyst happens very quickly, deftly, almost as if it was not said. The act is more important than the content: here we see the use of speech for voyeuristic entry into the other.

Indeed, it is possible to understand this very quick entry into the analyst's inner world as the verbal equivalent of a visual activity.

Given her career as a cinematographer, we may see here 'has anyone ever offered that to you?' as a photo-shoot – an attempt to view her analyst's inner world.

Analyst:
It makes me wonder if you're thinking about the voyeuristic part of being a therapist.

Annie:
You're right. I hadn't thought of that. You hear back whole descriptions of people's experience. That's interesting. But it's for a different purpose – at least we hope so. That immediately brings up how people have been commenting on how voyeuristic my new work is. I'm doing houses in neighbourhoods, especially the windows. Usually I get a reflection, but it feels a little like an encroachment sometimes. I've been filming a lot this week.

The patient, through the analyst's help, then discusses her voyeurism and how she is not making reflective films but encroaching on people's lives. She is following up, through free association, the act of encroaching upon the analyst's inner world. She knows that she has not used the analytic object for reflective purposes – as a blank screen – but has breached the analytic mirror. And we know that a 'mirror' is an important object from her childhood, when she would look at her reflection in the window to see if it moved.

If one believed this was a moment to interpret, one might say, 'It is interesting, isn't it, how your thoughts on encroaching upon the window rather than using it for reflective purposes follow on from your effort to enter my internal world – as if you are asking us to think about the different ways of relating to an other.' This kind of interpretation follows the analysand's logic of thought, it derives from her and when stated it should be clear, consciously, how the link is made. It also picks up an important line of thought having to do with the analysand's penetration of the other – something that she emphasises when she reports having invaded James's email.

Analyst:
We talked a good deal on Friday about how you expect I will feel threatened by your thoughts of me having a family, as if there's a danger or 'watch out' in the air.

Annie:
It's different between you and Marcus. With him it was more of an overwhelm. I plugged into all the difficulties there would be with him having a family, including ones that aren't even on the table, like the fact that his teenage boys know more scholastically than I do. Now that I'm getting clearer about it, there's Marcus's mind in front of me and I get to have access to it. With your family it felt more like I might destroy something, not meaning to. But at the same time maybe I want to a little bit. You have a wife, so to interject myself there would be to destroy something.

The session concludes with Annie's interest in Marcus's mind, her rivalry with his children, and her fear that she could destroy the analyst's family if she were to 'interject' herself there.

Analyst:
And Marcus doesn't have a wife any more.

Annie:
I'm afraid I'd get in there and mess it all up. Mess up what he's built with his children and the lives they have. Like I'm a cancer.

Returning to the drive-line of thought, Annie says that if she were to interject herself in the family she would 'mess it up'; she repeats the word 'mess', concluding that she is like 'a cancer'. Thus the session begins with a good mess or messing, and ends with a bad mess or messing.

Discussion

The session ends with a series of statements that imply questions. Annie says, of her relation to Marcus, 'I'm afraid I'd get in there and mess it all up . . . Like I'm a cancer.'

How does this link with the material of the session? At the beginning Annie is describing how she liberates a plant from its pot, and how this allows her to make a mess and have fun. Later she thinks she has liberated her analyst from his bog and that he has new colour. What does this apparently creative making-of-a-mess have to do with being destructive and with being a cancer? Annie has fun making a mess, but this childlike mess-making seems to ruin the object.

This material then joins with a transference line of thinking. She would need to find a man who is trapped in a pot – perhaps the analyst, rooted in the pot of the analytic chair – and her task would be to set him free. In that way, she could both free him and have him at the same time. So Annie is 'curing' her analyst through talk, telling him stories aimed to enliven him. He is trapped, but Annie can transport him out of this realm into a wider, freer earth. We might wonder whether the aunt's story of Pandora, who was also a talker, helped liberate Annie from the maternal grandmother who was bogging her down in her anality. Her aunt may have narrated this story – passing it from her mother to her sister's daughter – to liberate herself from being full of shit.

At the same time the communication tells us of the *form* of Annie's thinking: while buying a plant she figures things out and thinks of finding someone like her analyst. In the course of an action a thought arises.

This shows how action can be a constituent of unconscious thinking. In bringing the plant into her home she is also bringing home her analyst, because she has linked them in her thoughts. However, mid-way through the hour Annie tries to enter the analyst's mind. She intrudes upon him. Then she ends with a fear of destructive entry into familial situations.

I think the cancer, here, represents the voyeuristic excitement generated by anal-intrusiveness. Her grandmother was intruding into her body to get her shit out, something that caused her excitation, and Annie is excited to discover the kind of shit that others have hidden inside them. So, although she begins the hour with something of an idealised planting of the anal self, then associates to a good analyst with good colour, she ends up feeling she is cancerous because that anal-self is interrupted by a voyeuristic attachment, something she enacts in the session.

Her line of thought also articulates a form of memory. When Annie was a toddler her grandmother interpreted her anal functioning as infectious. She gave her suppositories to cleanse her out and then wiped her bottom in ways that merged the grandmother's dread of faecal bacteria with her excitement over its origins. The grandmother unconsciously communicated this to Annie over the years so that Annie now identifies with getting people to give up their shit, which she finds exciting, but which she also associates with cancer. It is cancerous on two counts: it is the source of that malignancy that her grandmother tried to wipe out; but it has metastasised through its attachment to sexuality, as she now *desires* to do this. Hence if Annie enters a relationship she will spread her malignancy and endanger those around her.

The analyst contains this action; he does not interpret it per se, but allows Annie to continue. Thus he allows her to express her anal-intrusiveness without reproach. We might ask why.

A few thoughts about the transference and projective identification.

It is clear that Annie thinks, in part, transferentially. That is, she uses the transference to conjure a relationship that constitutes a form of thought through object usage. Of this she seems aware, probably partly due to the analyst's interpretations but also, I expect, because relating to the other is essential to her cure.

In the order of projection as a form of thinking, Annie tells us that in idealising Marcus she is, according to Carlos, diminishing herself. We see a transference line of thought but we also see that she uses Carlos to think a thought about her analyst; that is, she goes out into the world for what we might term 'accessory thinking'. Accessory thinking uses objects and others to symbolically process, and contain, mental complexities. In this session Annie also projectively identifies the part of her that feels diminished (due to her idealisation) by getting Carlos to feel stupid. She brings it about in him, tells him he should think of his mother, and urges him to take all of this to his analyst. This circuitry of the projective also moves in and out of the transference as she tells her analyst that he needs to look at her relation to her mother to understand why she feels so diminished.

This is all quite obvious, but what I wish to emphasise is the patient's unconscious *skill* in projecting. She is specific and coherent, and maintains a line of thought in the projective realm. There is no severe splitting of self and other, and we see her using the projective line of thought in a creative manner. Such a skill indicates a high level of psychic creativity and unconscious cooperation with psychoanalysis. She is aware that she must convey what ails her to the analyst. She uses projection, projective identification and the transference to map out unconscious answers to the questions she poses.

Let us review the session in brief. Annie figures out, while buying a pot plant, that it is best to allow the other to figure things out for himself rather than to impose one's own views. She buys the plant and thinks of finding someone like her analyst; then over the weekend she liberates the plant from the pot. We can see a clear line of thought. Having narrated the tale of persecuting Carlos over the weekend, she figures out that she should not dominate him in this way and allows him to figure things out for himself. This thought occurs in the act of buying a plant that needs liberation from its confinement so that it can grow more freely. At the same time she thinks of finding someone like her analyst. That is, she wants to find someone who will liberate her from her confinement and allow her to grow.

This quest must be understood in light of the problems in her own growth. We may imagine that, for Annie, her grandmother was someone who watched her grow every day, measuring her body, making sure to give her suppositories so that she would grow properly. Growth meant evacuation dictated by the other, and her life was confined within the other's cloying fantasy.

What is Annie trying to figure out?

What is there about analysis that has allowed her to grow? Given that Annie feels she is full of shit needing evacuation, how has analysis transformed this view of the self, so that now her bottom is something that could settle into the earth in order that she could grow more naturally and in a less confined manner?

At the same time there is another question: how can she understand her voyeuristic entry into the other – whether in her work, in her viewing of James's email or in her attempted entry into the analyst?

Perhaps we can see that Annie is something of a laparoscopic suppository. The grandmother's suppositories looked inside Annie and found – so far as Annie was concerned – things to excite her. (Recall that she came to orgasm during such administrations.) So looking *into* the other *in a forced way* is presumably to bring about a sexual state of mind in the other.

The question?

It is posed in the transference: 'I have told you about looking into others and I have looked into you in the session, but you do not feel penetrated or excited. Why not?'

We shall see how this question, and others, are pursued in the following sessions.

Session 2 (Tuesday)

Annie:
I was thinking about what we talked about at the end yesterday. It seems right. I was taken back to what my psychologist said to me at nineteen years old – that I felt I was responsible for my parents' divorce. I heard that, but I didn't yet see how it transformed into how I acted with Marcus. Everything is there.

Carlos said to me, 'When I talk about politics, you tune out.' I said, 'Yes, I do space out.' He asked me why and I thought about my dad.

Before considering the logic of free-associative sequence in this session, let us look at the form of the early contents.

Annie says she was 'thinking' about what had been 'talked about' in the Monday session. She says it 'seems right' and indeed it springs a memory of what her psychologist said to her at the age of nineteen.

The contiguity of the words 'thinking', 'talked about' and 'seems' in such a short space (delivered, I shall presume, with a certain affective conviction) would appear to be evidence, so far as signifiers go, of thinking, talking and feeling. But Annie concludes her opening remark with the statement 'Everything is there.' Everything? The feeling one might get is that she is being glib.

Note how many objects she uses in just a few seconds. First there is the analyst; she thinks about what they talked about. Then she refers to what her psychologist said when she was nineteen. Then she refers to Marcus and that she cannot see how the psychologist's observation transformed how she acted with Marcus. Then she talks about Carlos and what he said. The analyst, the psychologist, Marcus, Carlos and then her father: five objects in almost as many seconds.

When she continues by saying 'Carlos said to me . . .' she gives us another order of unconscious articulation: projection. She is now inside the Carlos narrator. What we hear from Annie, she has heard from Carlos; so we, the listener, are now inside the Carlos object.

When Carlos asked her about why she tunes out, and she reports that it brought her father to her mind, the order of projection converges with the order of the transference, because Carlos is now a stand-in for the function of the analyst.

The theme is that she 'spaces out', and we can see Annie enacting the very thing she is talking about – by creating a parallel analysis that allows her to be one step removed from the real deal.

There was the blowout at the dinner table every night between him and my stepmother and her friend. Night after night the argument got too heated. Politics,

The patient talks about overhearing the 'blowout' at the dinner table every night, between father and stepmother. Annie shifts to this being 'night after night' and by evoking the to me, represents anger. The other thing is, my stepmother. I don't know much about Buddhism, but her way of practising it was to lord it over us. Marcus is a Buddhist. He's casual in his practice. And he has three sons. And he is a maths prodigy.

night she moves beyond the table to the bedroom.

Politics, she says, represents anger, and this unit of association ends with the comment that Marcus is casual in his practice of Buddhism, has three sons, and is a maths prodigy. The logic of this last set of associations might be that the maths he is casual with is intercourse, that he can produce three kids. We may consider that the rhythmic 'night after night' is both an allusion to the sexuality in the night and to the action – it is a small speech act – and the conclusion that the more relaxed self can produce more children.

What might the questions be inside these associations? We know that her stepmother's child was a stillbirth. So these associations may be following this line of thought: 'I space out of politics (that is, family life) because if I spaced in I would be invaded by the image of destructive intercourse that produces dead babies.'

In my first marriage, my husband spent a lot of time with his mother after his father died during our honeymoon.

The line of thought – 'intercourse kills' – continues in the next set of associations as she thinks about her first marriage and the death of her husband's father 'during our honeymoon'.

For this patient, death-inside-a-container is a line of thought that makes the father's death during (inside) the honeymoon of extra significance. The father is killed during the ritual of sexual consummation: that is, the children who have sex now kill the father.

I wanted to pull away and be a satellite. I didn't know how to be anything else. That's why I feel I might mess it up. I talked to Marcus last night. We're set to

In the discussion below we will examine in some detail the associations that follow. But let us simply note here Annie's sequence of thought.

have lunch a week from tomorrow. That gives me way too much time to think about things. I'm getting the cyst off tomorrow.

I felt like a satellite at the family reunion last summer. People didn't seem to want to get into it. I was talking with my stepmum and her maid came into the room to check on her to see if she was okay! It feels like if I *were* accepted, I wouldn't know what to do with it, wouldn't know how to act. Marcus seems to desperately need to touch something. Not physically. He has that hole where his wife used to be. There was a lot of conversation every day and now no one's there. He asked if he could come down and see my marigold.

Tess came over yesterday. She did four hours of film editing. It was helpful. She seems alive now, versus when I taught her. She told me about the surgery she had: she had excess skin cut off. Then the drainage tubes got infected. Then the antibiotics led to grand mal seizures. Now she looks bright and alive. She's normal weight but has these huge scars.

A pause of a few minutes follows before Annie continues.

When Carlos and I went through that at the weekend I was getting that feeling about me – as toxic.

Analyst:
What is it like?

Annie:
Like rather than being the kind of person who supports, I try to hold them back. Unwittingly, I figure out their issues and play on them. This is an overt example: Maggie is

I become a satellite because I do not know how to be.

To be would be to mess things up.

Knowing of something in advance, I think too much.

I am getting rid of the cyst (of something I could otherwise think too much about).

I was a satellite last summer.

Because people did not want to get into me.

The maid rescued the mother from me (as I was trying to get into her).

However, if I were accepted I would not know what to do.

Marcus needs to touch but has a hole in him, due to loss.

We used to fill up our losses with conversation, but now there is a hole again.

If talking is rejected, maybe we can use sight and seeing as a substitute.

Tess talked a lot about a hole in herself. Talking helps to cure holes.

But one can talk too much and be toxic.

Annie's sequence of thought here is that by talking she adheres to people. In fact, she 'holds' on to them by going to their sore points and playing on them. (She is just beginning to realise why she has adopting a child. She went in, was tested, and was told she has a 'horned uterus'. Depending on how it's horned it can be okay or dangerous for having a child. After that, I heard she was trying to adopt, but I haven't talked to her about it. Then I had another conversation with someone in James's apartment building, called Susan, who was telling me all about the fibroids in her uterus. Loudly. She then left down the hallway to find her boyfriend and it turns out he'd been sitting right around the corner listening to her talk about her uterus looking like a gourd. I later told Maggie about this conversation with Susan and as soon as the words came out, I realised how insensitive it was, even though I was using the conversation to illustrate how obnoxiously loud Susan was. Subconsciously, I do this to people – that's why I'm toxic.

Analyst:
You talk about your feelings as though they are so intertwined with other people's lives that it's as though you have some responsibility . . .

Annie:
I see that with the one big fight my parents had when I was eleven, that made me feel responsible for the divorce. My father stayed in the area for a year or so and then moved pretty far away, to Wales. I must have felt there was nothing I could do to keep him here. I wasn't enough. Therefore I had to have done something wrong. Had I done it right, he would've stayed. I think he may still feel some guilt about it. I don't think we talked on the

driven Marcus away: she played on the sore point of his loss.)

Note how many conversations Annie reports to follow, as if she is filling the hour with too much conversation.

She ends this set of associations with a remarkable statement: 'I later told Maggie about this conversation with Susan and as soon as the words came out, I realised how insensitive it was . . . I do this to people – that's why I'm toxic.' Talking means that toxic things come out of her mouth.

Importantly, the analyst picks up the theme of 'talking' in order to be intertwined with people.

In response to the interpretation Annie turns to the topic of her father and says, 'I don't think we talked on the phone much after he left' and then, 'I may have been hard to talk to on the phone – not much to say.' So we see here the fantasy that if she had been able to talk to the father then this action might have adhered to him, kept her in touch with him in more than one way. But listen carefully to what she says next: 'My self as a child was watching and quiet.' This is by way of consciously phone much after he left, but I don't really have memory of it. I may have been hard to talk to on the phone – not much to say. My self as a child was watching and quiet.

Analyst:
You portray it as manipulative, but from the sound of it, with Carlos over the weekend, you didn't have to do much to tap into that in him.

Annie:
That's right, there was definitely projection going on with that. When he told his analyst about it, apparently they talked about how his last relationship that failed had the same push–pull as he had with his mother. He said, 'leave me alone', but if she did he wasn't okay with that either. It was the first time I saw a glimmer of him saying *he'd* done something to *her*. So it was interesting. I suppose the thought to consider is that I'm not God, to be as toxic as I think I am.

Did you ever see that movie, *Badlands*? Sissy Spacek and Martin Sheen. They're young and he kills her father to get her, so they end up on the road as waifs, being looked for and hiding. And they get into situations where he keeps killing. She is horrified by it but sticks with him. I've thought about this a lot, that the evil in the world is often a combination of two. Like Myra Hindley and her lover. Something was created by the two of them that brought out this . . . I think when I'm . . . When I look at James, did we freeze each other? Is who I am part of what threw him into the rigidity? We went in a toxic

telling us why she did not talk, but we note that lack of speech is compensated by vision. So if we reverse this we can say that talking, for Annie, is seeing; she talks to see into the person and in turn to be seen by the other.

The analyst understands her verbal account – 'portray' – but uses his feelings to disagree with her: 'from the sound of it . . .'

Annie agrees with this reading of the emotional subtext derived from the analyst's use of his feelings.
    The analyst's different view is unconsciously interpreted by Annie to indicate that her views are not omnipotent. She rethinks her relation to Carlos and is relieved to recognise she is not a toxic God.
    Having established this, however, she will then go on to prompt the analyst to return to the destructive aspect of her personality.

Her associations take her to the film *Badlands* and to the murderer Myra Hindley, to a relationship in which evil is the combination of two bad people. This continues the line of thought that the primal scene is destructive.
    From here she goes on to think of aspects of her family history.

direction rather than moving in another direction. I don't know. A lot of things reinforced it. The divorce, my father leaving, my mother's treatment of me. I was too sexual with other kids at school. But I wasn't toxic with my half-brothers ever, though my stepmother thought I was.

Analyst:
We've talked about this for a long time up till now without calling it this.

Annie:
Last year, intensely so. I thought you were starting a new family and there were changes in the schedule [of sessions]. My feelings were strong about wanting you, and while you were starting a family I wasn't and couldn't. It's backwards. I wanted you to drop that and be with me – yet that would have been the toxic thing. It's funny, I feel really sleepy.

Analyst:
What do you make of it?

Annie:
It's a shutdown. Everything gets so heavy. Visiting my dad's family, I'd sleep a lot. I wanted the day to go by so I wouldn't have to be in it. Overload. Something to do with being a teenager too. I disappeared. Maybe that's what the sleep is. I could disappear. Because if I'm not there people won't have to go away. If I don't do anything then things won't change. In my nightmares I was worried about my mum being taken away and being left with nothing. Maybe this has to do with the mirror also. The mirror was moving when I wasn't, which

Annie now moves from her own family's history to the analyst's formation of his family.

She has started to feel sleepy and she associates this to visiting her father's family, making the interesting statement 'I wanted the day to go by so I wouldn't have to be in it. Overload.'
Then she tells us that she 'disappeared'. In fact, her sleepiness in this moment is a form of such disappearing, an emotional experience evoked within the transference as she tries to think of sexual life.
Next Annie talks about nightmares with her mother disappearing and she recalls the 'mirror' event (looking at her

meant that I couldn't control something. But I was also inert. Since I couldn't control it, I had to be inert or I would lose my mother too. That goes with the dream where I'm a larva.

reflection in the window when she was a child). She thinks of the mirror, although interestingly here her associations are about confusion, not of self with the image, but with the container – with the mirror itself. 'The mirror was moving when I wasn't' is what she says, but she probably meant to say that the *image* in the mirror was moving when she wasn't.

She links the mirror to maternal abandonment. To the maternal other-as-mirror, leaving her if she isn't still. She has to silence her instincts (sexuality) if she is to keep her mother, and now others. Again, ironically, by splitting off her affects and her instincts (to be satellites from herself) she can preserve relationships.

This links with the larva dream, which represents a scene of birth without the presence of the parents. Mother and father insect have gone. The self is born alone.

Analyst:
If you weren't there at least things wouldn't get worse.

Annie:
Right. I was scared to do or say *anything*. I think that goes with why I was trying to hide my broken arm: 'I'm not injured, go away, don't pay attention!' It made me noticeable.

The session ends, ten minutes late.

Discussion

Let us look in more detail at Annie's line of thinking about being a satellite in a social group.

We can see here what I term a 'vivid' free association. Such associations are like riddles. The patient says that she wanted to be a satellite and then says, 'I didn't know how to be anything else.' She then says, by way of unconscious explanation, 'That's why I feel I might mess it up.' I think she is unconsciously communicating the experience that after the death of her father-in-law, when her husband turned to his mother, Annie had to pull away and be a satellite for fear that if she had said what she thought, she would have messed up her relationship with her husband.

We note a continuation of the anal line of thought from the Monday session. The toddler Annie understandably interpreted her grandmother's actions to mean that her anal messing was responsible for driving away both her mother, who was off lecturing, and her father, who was working very long hours for his parish.

However, inside this ordinary communication there are sustained syntactical relations that also provide evidence for other lines of thinking. The patient could simply have said that she wanted to pull away, but she likens this to being a 'satellite': a non-human object. When she says 'I didn't know how to be anything else' she indicates that her existence is now linked to being a 'thing', evident both in the structure of her language – 'anything' – and in the image of the satellite. In this respect I think she is recalling a period of contained psychosis in which, in order to eliminate her anger from the scene, she has to reduce herself to a non-human thing-being.

We could find more associations to the word 'satellite' and to other words that lie within it. 'Sat' and 'light' are the two most obvious of these, but the sound of 'settle' is also immanent in the sound of 'satellite'. We have observed how verbally fast-moving, glib and light Annie can be in a session. We have noticed that she says 'go away, don't pay attention', 'it made me noticeable.' What must it have been like for a child, year after year after year, to be given laxatives and sat on the toilet to poo? Would this potentially humiliating and laborious moment not eventually give rise to her wish to get it over with quickly – not to 'settle'? Does this help us to understand why this intelligent, deep-thinking woman might at times seem to evacuate thoughts in a light manner, refusing to settle into issues? When she senses that life is about to put her on the toilet, to get her to evacuate her feelings (in the situation of a 'loaded' family reunion, for example), even if she feels anguished at becoming a satellite, might this not also be a wish? Given the alternatives – to sit heavy or to sit light, to evacuate or to stay removed – Annie has a choice to make almost every time she has a significant encounter with the other. As we have discussed, sometimes she keeps her thoughts to herself, other times she spills them out.

If we return to Monday's session, we see that Annie feels bad about her aggressiveness towards Carlos and, as they work together on the studio, she realises she 'should let him figure it out for himself'. In other words, she knows that she should not continue a pattern of intrusion and should give Carlos his own space. Interestingly, the very next thing she says is, 'Spatially, he does have limits on how he thinks and I think very well spatially.' So we have two references to space (the environment of a satellite) and to figuring out space.

This theme is pursued in the Tuesday session when Annie finds herself talking about how she occupied space in her family. And she and Carlos continue to pursue their own work on this issue. She reports that Carlos says she 'tunes out' when he discusses politics and Annie agrees, saying that yes, she 'spaces out'. Together they are working out her difficulty with conflict, whether it be the politics of family or with other familiar objects. Her solution is to tune out or space out.

As Lacan has shown, words are signifiers that sound like other signifiers. Were we to have access to a printed account of Annie's entire analysis we would find words releasing sounds (other words) that established a chain of signifiers that would, from Lacan's point of view, constitute the voice of 'the subject'. For Lacan, this is the articulation of the Other and it is an important form of unconscious thinking – though not, of course, the only one. I included my associations to the word 'satellite', taking time to dwell on a single word, in order to show how it can weave into the categories of the memorial, the instinctual, the relational and the emotional, but also to indicate how the psychoanalyst's own unconscious *dream-works* the material. The patient's words play upon the analyst's mind all the time, signifiers linking to other signifiers both in the analysand's speaking and in our own silent parallel discourse. This is no more than saying, with Freud, that the analyst's unconscious 'catches the drift of the patient's unconscious', but with the important addition that the analyst's unconscious will play an *actively* associative role of its own during this engagement.

It is interesting to note that in the week following these sessions Annie continued to use the metaphor of being a 'satellite'. In the context of one of the subsequent sessions, the cluster of associative connections gave the signifier an additional meaning when the analyst 'heard' the phrase 'sad light'. He used his association to the word and spoke what he heard, and this made both logical and emotional sense to the analysand.

Let us look now at three enigmatic sentences that Annie utters in sequence. She says: 'That gives me way too much time to think about things. I'm getting the cyst off tomorrow. I felt like a satellite at the family reunion last summer.' Removal of the cyst has turned up in many areas following its introduction, but there is also a pre-association, in the word 'blowout'. Recall that she 'spaced' out of family matters due to the 'blowout at the dinner table every night'. We remember the sequence as one of not wanting to think for a week about Marcus, then the brief mention of the removal of the cyst, then the statement about feeling she is a satellite at the family event.

Let me put this into an interpretation that might help us think about it: 'You have talked about worrying too long about Marcus, but you slide very quickly past the worry of having the cyst out, as if you are saying, "Oh, I haven't been worrying about that worry!" – but by removing yourself from the worry you may become a satellite to your inner feelings.'

We can see here another line of thought – a chain of action of sorts – that occurs simultaneously with the many references to objects coming out of the self. In the first sentence of the session Annie mentions talking: 'thinking about what we talked about at the end of yesterday'. We then recall the section of the session on the talking-blowouts of the parents. All the while, as she tells her associations to the analyst, she also recounts a parallel talking to Marcus or Carlos. Let's hear again the many references to talking, in order of presentation:

1. I *talked* to Marcus last night.
2. I was *talking* with my stepmum.
3. There was a lot of *conversation* every day and now no one's there.
4. [Tess] *told* me about the surgery.
5. I heard [Maggie] was trying to adopt, but I haven't *talked* to her about it.
6. Then I had *another conversation* with someone in James's apartment building.
7. Susan . . . was *telling* me all about the fibroids.
8. *Loudly*.
9. Her boyfriend [was] . . . *listening to her talk* about her uterus.
10. I later *told* Maggie.

After Annie tells us of her fear of something toxic coming out of her mouth she simultaneously talks about all the people to whom she has talked. This is highly overdetermined. She creates scenes of talking and of the talking self. At the same time there are people overhearing; there is what is heard, but there is also the cumulative effect upon the listener of the act of hearing. Pandora opened a box which she was meant to keep closed. It contained undisclosed objects given to her by the gods, and her curiosity caused a plague.

Annie draws our attention to her view, inspired by the operation, that she contains toxins that are released through talking. She cannot stop herself from talking . . . and she is now inside the 'talking cure'. She proceeds to elaborate unconsciously one of the determinants of talking, as if she is asking herself *why* she talks – what purpose talking serves, other than communicating mental contents.

Her associations take her to another malignant pair in *Badlands*, a film in which outcasts exact revenge by killing a father. She fears pairing with Marcus as her cancerous self will kill him and his family. She is relieved by the analytic boundary that protects self and other from a murderous sexuality that otherwise would kill the analyst's partner and family. The logic? This Pandora-woman contains evil shit-sexuality that if paired with other shits would kill the fathers and destroy the paternal order.

Let's think now about the moment in the session where Annie becomes sleepy. The 'overload' that makes the self sleepy is about having to take in too much (shit). Shutting the self down is a defence against potential retaliation – that is, shitting on the other. Note the logic of sequence in the following: 'I disappeared. Maybe that's what the sleep is. I could disappear. Because if I'm not there people won't have to go away.' Overloaded, angry, on the verge of pairing with other shits if I sleep and disappear, if I remove myself from others they will not abandon me. Annie thus teaches us that by dissociating from the family, by becoming a satellite, she is able to *preserve* a relationship with people whom otherwise she fears she will repel or infect.

Let us return to Annie's phrase, 'My self as a child was watching and quiet.' Here the particular arrangement of her wording, what we would term her syntactical structure, is striking. Syntax, the peculiar way a speaker works within the rules of grammar, is a separate line of unconscious thinking. (For example, whilst the subject matter of a play or a novel will contain many, many lines of thought, the way words flow, the way sentences are structured, the way thoughts are patterned: these all form a separate category from the semantic realm.)

We can see that Annie's syntax articulates a split self: 'my self as a child'. The split self has two separate verbal qualities: it is 'watching and quiet'. Now we know she is referring to a time of great trauma when in fact she could not speak due to great mental pain. In this very brief wording, her syntax in itself articulates the pain and the split in the self. It also provides a potential clue to the child looking in the 'mirror' window. Her memory is that in looking into the mirror the image moved when she did not. What she recalls, I think, is that she attempted to be both the looker and the looked-upon at the same time. She denies her own movement but it is projected into the image: it is the image that moved. The effort to be in two places at once produces an anxiety – an anxiety that she recalls so intensely because she *was* in two places at once. This links to her subsequent voyeuristic aim to look into James, to wonder about his inner reality.

Unusually, in this session the analyst runs over time. Can we trace the unconscious ideas that might make this a logical act on his part? Has 'time' figured in the hour?

The patient gives a picture of family conflict that seemed endless and that emptied her mind. This may be seen as a communication that, as a child, she did not have time to think through what was going on. She refers directly to the unbearableness of the passing of time – having to wait a week to see Marcus, a pain that may well be made up to her by the analyst who is present and gives her more time. Annie also refers directly to the disappearance of her father, implicitly asserting that she did not have enough time with him. She then goes over well-worn issues, dredging up familiar themes; the analyst points out: 'We've talked about this for a long time up till now without calling it this.' It is not clear to us what is meant here by 'it', but I think analyst and patient understand 'it'. The word 'toxic' is repeated several times, like a drum beat, and after a few more associations Annie becomes sleepy. The analyst asks her what she makes of it. We can conjecture that the patient has a sense that time is up and is aware that the analyst has not ended the session. In response to his question about her sleepiness – 'What do you make of it?' – she replies, 'It's a shutdown.' I think the word 'shutdown' refers, in part, to the end of the hour. We could track the logic of her subsequent associations, but she moves to the fear of her mother being taken away from her. Is it possible that her analyst has gone over time because he is waiting for something not yet spoken but lingering? Does this patient have a need to go over time, to go beyond the expectable and the controllable into another realm in order to talk about the disappearing mother? And what are we to make of her final set of associations to her broken arm? She says she tried to hide this, quoting herself – 'I'm not injured, go away, don't pay attention!' – and explaining that it made her 'noticeable'. Is she feeling that the analyst is staying too long because of her injuries? Does this kind of visibility evoke an anxiety in her?

If we consider the poetics of Annie's session (the form of her delivery) it might appear at times to be rather manic. Important signifiers are brought out for verbal view – thinking, talking, sensing – and she also makes use of memory. The quick movement through her various objects has a speed to it that, combined with her sometimes glib conclusions, could indicate a –K frame of mind.[35]

But what do we mean by 'manic', and can we be sure that this is an appropriate concept here? Annie's comments display several mental qualities – fastness, brevity, shallowness, charm, irony – that could imply a manic presentation. In fact, however, the material that follows is so rich in detail that I believe something else is at work here. Annie's 'everything' announces the presence of *intense condensation*. Thus one way of differentiating between these two very opposite kinds of thinking – manic and condensed – is to observe whether such thinking is meaningful. Does it, as we see here with Annie, release further rich material, or is it followed by empty speech?

Let's look at how the Tuesday session elaborates, free-associatively, on the Monday hour. What line of thought do we see being followed? To think in this way requires us to function on a different level. We have to pull back from the minute details of our microanalysis, in order to abstract broader psychic themes.

One of these may be put this way, as a question. On Monday Annie asks herself why it is that she cannot find someone like her analyst. She concludes by saying she is a cancerous mess. In the Tuesday session, when talking about Maggie, Susan and others, she says in passing, 'rather than being the kind of person who supports, I try to hold them back. Unwittingly, I figure out their issues and play on them'.

On Monday she reports a talking weekend with Carlos when he felt she had accused him of being stupid – clearly his Achilles heel. Later in that session Annie penetrates the analyst with a question about his voyeurism, putting the analyst in a vulnerable position. So the first action with Carlos constitutes projective identification, whilst the second is a transference enactment of her messing with people. On Tuesday she goes much, much further in terms of her development of these insights. Now she actually says that she is cruel to people by playing on what she perceives as their weaknesses.

Annie's conscious conclusion, however, leaves out her crucial unconscious interpretation of why she plays on others' weaknesses. Recall in the session the link between talking with Marcus as a way of filling up the holes in their lives: gaps created by lost objects. When she reports her feeling that talking was toxic she adds that she tries to 'hold people back'. Her analyst comments that she talks as though her feelings are 'intertwined with other people's lives'.

Annie can see her own cruelty but she misses the unconscious reason why she plays upon the sore points in other people's characters. It is her attempt to hold on to them, to maintain contact, and if this means hurting them – so be it.

Should one put this to the analysand? At the appropriate moment, of course, this would be correct, but here we see evidence that Annie is thinking this through herself and therefore it would not be right for the analyst to make it explicit. Ironically, the notion that consciousness is liberating is not always so true. There can be times when consciousness would actually interfere with unconscious thinking, which, if left to itself, will develop more insight and enable further psychic change.

Finally, let us return to the questions we asked at the end of Monday's session. We have inferred from the chain of ideas that Annie is posing a question (among many) that asks: 'Why, when I penetrate you with the voyeuristic aim to find the shit in you, do you not find this exciting? And why does this make me feel better?'

" ucs, left to itself, will develop..." ?

In Tuesday's session Annie talks about how Marcus 'has that hole where his wife used to be' – one that she obviously talks to him a lot about: 'There was a lot of conversation every day and now no one's there.' Annie's next set of free associations are about Tess and her surgery. 'The drainage tubes got infected. Then the antibiotics led to grand mal seizures. Now she looks bright and alive.'

It is not possible to hear Annie talking about 'that hole' in Marcus without the anus coming to mind. We also know that Annie talks in order to enter people to find out the shit within them. But in the case of Marcus, her effort to enter his hole to find out what was going on inside him did not work; indeed, it repelled him.

As we know, Annie's conclusion is that talking drives away the other and if she is to stop people leaving her she must remain in hiding. What she is discovering in the transference, however, is that by entering the analyst's hole (or holes) she does not excite him. Her analyst makes a crucial interpretation, that she talks to intertwine herself with people. In arriving at this insight – which the analyst reported as simply occurring to him without any premeditation – Annie is offered insight into why she talks. Her grandmother's anal intrusions were exciting and have led Annie to attach drive and excitation to forms of speech in which she intrudes. However, on an even more fundamental level, this was the only way she could remain in contact with this important mothering person – to ensure that she was not abandoned. Thus her need for the relationship superseded the excitation.

Session 3 (Wednesday)

Annie:
I feel much better today. I went to film after yesterday's session but I couldn't. I felt the light wasn't right. It was too hot and nothing was presenting itself. And I was still tired. So I went home and had a nap. Then I went to class. I enjoyed it. Only four of the seven students were there. The missing

The session begins with a continuation of certain lines of thought: of being tired, sleeping, and something missing (the missing students).

Annie notes that the previous session went over time by ten minutes. She wonders why, but says she appreciates it. Nonetheless, her first comments tell us about her state ones were all juniors. It was actually very nice. I was very concrete with them. I told them: 'I'm giving you a specific assignment – if you do it, you get an A; if you don't, you get an F. The assignment is to go to the art library and find a painting, any painting, that is new to you, bring it in and say what struck you.' *(pauses)* I don't know if you went over time yesterday on purpose because things were intense or if you made a mistake, but I was glad it happened. In those few minutes, a lot went on. I kind of appreciated it, mistake or not. My first concern was whether someone was out there waiting. If I'd had to wait ten minutes I'd have been upset. That leads to two other thoughts: the students last night wanted to stay past 10 p.m. editing their films. It was nice they wanted to stick around. Also, I talked to Marcus this morning. He told me how his middle child was helping the youngest with his Latin lessons. They were really involved in it. Then the oldest came into the room and they ignored him. So he went back out and did this comical thing with Marcus where he went on and on saying, 'I'm invisible! What if I went to school and no one could see me!' He's so social he couldn't bear it, but his little brother could. Funny he brought that up after our session, where I'd talked about being invisible.

To make it too simple: being with James let me stay in a comfortable–uncomfortable position of being invisible. It's interesting that when Mum died that position was no longer possible. Something in my connection with her made me need to be invisible.

of mind after the session – that she could not film, that she was too hot and tired and then took a nap and attended her class where there were students missing. This links with a feeling that it overloaded her, that she was over-heated (excited) by so much shit coming out of her, so she had to put herself to sleep. As we will see, however, it was an essential overload.

Perhaps the analyst stayed over time because he wanted to.

Soon she is asking an unconscious question about her invisibility. She begins with a comment by Marcus's son, then her observation that being with James let her be invisible, then her comment that when her mother died 'that position' – of being invisible – was 'no longer possible'. (We shall return to the illogic of this comment.) She then says: 'Something in my connection with her made me need to be invisible.' It is at this point that the unconscious poses a question: 'What was there about my connection with my mother that made me need to be invisible?'

Annie's free associations seem to answer this question along two lines. First let us look again at the logic of sequence. I will repeat just two sentences: 'Something in my connection with her made me need to be invisible. Apparently, Tess has told all the teachers that she loves me, so now they're teasing me a little, saying: "What do you do that we don't do?"'

I would not intervene here in practice, but it is interesting to consider how might one interpret the logic of the unconscious here. It could be put like this: 'You have wondered what there was in your connection with your mother that

Apparently, Tess has told all the teachers that she loves me, so now they're teasing me a little, saying: 'What do you do that we don't do?'

Analyst:
And did you tell them?

Annie:
(smiling) I'm supposed to know this? If anything, she needs not to be told what to do, but to be asked for information. For example, instead of 'Why are you doing this?' it needs to be 'How can you do this; the emotion is not in the film – how can you get it in there?' Her first ideas always seem as if they're not going to work. Kind of silly.

She loves herons. She drives to the Fens and films them. Her

made you need to be invisible, and you followed this with a thought about how much Tess loves you. Might it be that it was your mother's love of you that you had to avoid; you had to be invisible so she could not see you and love you?' We know that Annie dreaded the moments when her mother would attempt to console her. So we rely here on a bit of history.

The mother was a *talker*, a political activist who could rant on and on. So to the last interpretive link we might add: 'You did not want mother to see into your thoughts, that you felt she was full of shit, which understandably you feared would lead to her abandonment of you.' It is relevant that her mother's mother has transmitted across the generations an idea that women need to be anally purged lest the shit come out of their mouths. Annie's mother could not stop talking, Annie is afraid that she too cannot stop and her grandmother's other female child (her aunt) tells her a story about a woman (Pandora) who cannot contain secrets.

But this is not the only line of thought sprung by the question 'Why do I make myself invisible around Mother?'

Annie responds further through her next free association as she discusses her student Tess, of whom she says 'she needs not to be told what to do'. I think this suggests the following question-and-answer: 'What was there in the connection that forced me to be invisible?' 'Had I been visible, Mother would have told me what to do.'

This line of thought is joined by another one that converges at this nodal point around the word teachers say: 'Why are you doing this? Maybe you shouldn't do birds', etc. I said: 'What do you like about herons?' She thought about it and figured it out: 'I've had a heron collection since I was four years old. The first time I saw one was with my grandfather. I was transfixed by the herons. He kept feeding me little sandwiches while I looked. It brings me back to my whole grandfather experience. That's what I'm trying to save and keep.' I said to her, 'Okay, how are you going to do this?' and she came up with: 'I'll make the photos and films of my collected herons into a documentary, and will give them a description, then pair my film with an official film of herons.' I told her, 'You know, it will probably work. You're juxtaposing kitsch and beauty, the memory and the actual.' So she has a way of taking a silly idea and making it into something substantial. The teachers are trying to make her process be like what they want it to be. I told her differently, that her process is what it is. That's why she went and told everyone she was in love with me.

Analyst:
You told her it's okay to go with her muse.

'invisible'. Tess has told other teachers that she loves Annie and these teachers now ask: 'What do you do that we don't do?' The analyst asks, 'And did you tell them?' – so we now have two explicit questions. The patient quite genuinely believes she does not know the answer to this question – 'I'm supposed to know this?' – but, typically with this kind of unconscious dialectic, she immediately answers the question by saying she is loved because she does not tell the student what to do. We can see here, from a theoretical vantage point, the emphasis Winnicott puts on potential space, the maternal holding environment, presentation of objects, and use of the object.

Of Tess, Annie says 'Her first ideas always seem as if they're not going to work'; this follows an observation that 'the emotion is not in the film – how can you get it in there?' In talking about Tess we see Annie also describing her own dilemma. How can she get deeper into 'things', how can she develop her emotional depths, given that she is a satellite orbiting object relations, rather than getting into them? Her answer is that she needs to begin with ideas that seem unworkable.

Annie describes Tess's love of herons, but actually this is a complex story of a girl's love of her grandfather. So to get deeper into things one needs to fall in love rather as a child does.

But you will have noted a separate line of thought within the story of Tess. In a fascinating way Annie records two questions, one right, the other wrong: 'Instead of "Why are you doing this?" it needs to be "How can you do this?"' Not blame, but empathic assistance. And

what are these process questions
about? 'The emotion is not in the
film – how can you get it in there?'
We have been following a line of
thought that expresses Annie's
unconscious knowledge of her
dissociation from object relations, of
a style of talking that is glib and fast-
moving, barely touching the depths.
Here she pursues this question and
tells herself how it is that she can
move from voyeuristic emotive
remove into an emotional fulfilment
of the photographed: that is, of the
representational world.

Her answer, unconsciously and
by proxy, is that she can do this
through the love and help of a
facilitating male other. She seeks to
recover a good marriage to the
father through the grandfather. This
is not a father through whom her
sexual aims will be destructive.
Relations to grandparents are almost
always a relation to the self with
parents who are above conflict: a
form of Oedipal transcendence.

Tess's story, then, can be seen as
a free-associative elaboration of, and
answer to, the problems of Annie's
remove from her mother. The other
she seeks, from whom she would not
be invisible, would have to be
someone who nurtured her and
allowed her to be a child.

A heron is a flying object but
one, interestingly, that likes to spend
a lot of time on the ground. It is close
enough for humans to observe it in
its natural environment. It is not a
satellite, permanently exiled to outer
space. The signifier 'heron' contains
the words 'here' and 'on'. We do not
know their significance for Tess, but
for satellite Annie a creature that can
fly but also be 'here', 'on' earth, has
special significance. Annie's inclusion
of this bird in the session and her

repetition of the name 'heron'
makes it into her own associative
object.

Annie:
Yes, and everyone else is confused. I
suspect that patients in analysis all
go through their own patterns and
it's a puzzle sometimes to try to
figure it out. There *is* a framework to
think about it in, but then you have
the *patient*, and it becomes a whole
different thing. I was going to ask
you . . . It's a funny question. I was
thinking about the process I've gone
through here, from the beginning.
The whole . . . metamorphosis, I
suppose. I was going to ask you if
there was a name for it.

Annie links her work with Tess to
being in analysis, so the transference
continues but supports other lines of
thought.
        She asks a question: how does
this process work?

Analyst:
How do you think of
'metamorphosis'?

Annie:
A change from one thing into
another – from larva to fully
functioning insect! *(smiles)* The
dreams I had of my being a larva . . . I
don't know if there's a psychological
concept for it, if you had to give it
a name. I'm interested in what *word*
you would use.

Analysis allows Annie to be larval, to
be cocooned in the presence of the
other (the grandfatherly being of the
analyst).

Analyst:
Honestly, my field tends to be dry
in this area; tends to think about
these things in a too-linear way.

The analyst cannot come up with a
beautiful word. His words remain
larval. But Annie-as-larva on the
verge of metamorphosis (birth into
good language) may be an image
that represents a faecal subject (larva
as stool-like; suppositories as larva)
on the verge of liberating herself
through language. Keeping in mind
her silencing of the self, not wording
what one feels, Annie is now putting
the previously unacceptable (shit)
into words. Not destructive,
malignant words, but language as a

creative avenue for the arrival of ideas and feelings. Thus she has transformed the significance of the larval object – from a purely cocooned object into a regressed being that is in a process of development.

Annie:

I've heard psychoanalysis can be 'finished', but there's also a continuing investigation. There's never a point where you get to the end because it's so complex. It's funny, there's the book I told you about once, *On Sleep*. It's about dreaming. My habit with books is that I often start two or three, put them aside, then finish them later. I couldn't believe what it was saying. The writer is a rock climber, a dream and visual researcher, Andrews maybe? It's interesting that he would think about it as a whole body–person engagement. Film-making is a little that way. He talks about vision. If you just take the physics of it, rods and cones are just a bunch of blobs. It takes a brain putting it together to see what you see. You learn from experience how to see. He's a lucid dreamer. He was amazed a dream could construct such rich visual experience. His interest was how much does the brain contribute to sight. Mice raised with no horizontal lines couldn't see them as adults!

Experience is so crucial to how you see. When I took my first hit of acid I wondered, 'Is my light blue someone else's light orange?' Experience may be different between people, so you actually can make films that are *yours* – personal.

Analyst:

Hm.

The intensity of this moment disseminates, as lines of thought that had converged now diverge. The word 'whole' reappears, as in the rock climber who thinks of what he does as a 'whole body–person engagement' which the patient links to photography. She is finding in her profession something that is making her feel more whole, rather than a hole.

Let us now consider a character feature that informs Annie's communications. Character is in itself a line of unconscious articulation.

First we have noted how there are sudden bursts of projection and projective identification when she thinks something through occupation of others. We have also noted manic-shallow mental movement that dispossesses her of a sense of emotional involvement and depth.

These lines of articulation, like all lines, are never silent but can recede and then return to the foreground. They return to centre stage when she discusses the book. Her first free association is that she often starts two or three books, then puts them aside before finishing them later. This is a way of discussing the manic idiom of her free associations.

In this frame of mind she lands on the thought that experience 'is so crucial to how you see' and moves on to taking acid, an example of a manic action that leads to a psychotic experience.

From this Annie comes to a conclusion, that 'experience may be different between people' – a remarkable statement, not because it is true, but because the word 'may' makes the obvious rather fragile. What if there were no differences? She concludes: 'so you actually can make films that are *yours* – personal'.

Annie:

His book seems like the pathway into that. The art school I teach at stresses the assignment, not what the student wishes to shoot. The book got really exciting to read. If I could see through someone else's eyes, how would it look? Suddenly I think you're disagreeing.

This line of thought continues with a question: 'If I could see through someone else's eyes, how would it look?' There is an affective immediate free association following this question. She says to her analyst: 'Suddenly I think you're disagreeing.'

Analyst:

What is your thought?

Annie:

You hesitated for a second when you said 'hm', as if you were turning it over and questioning it rather than accepting it, which is a reasonable thing to do I suppose.

Analyst:

I'm disappointed it came across that way and I think we should give some thought to this. It gets me wondering if you were maybe expecting disagreement.

Annie:

James would have to form his opinion and espouse it right there. Or say the same thing I just said in a different way. Or say no, then repeat what I said. It became his. Never 'that's interesting, what else did they say?' *Never, ever*.

James could not allow her a separate thought.

Analyst:

Almost as though you hadn't said anything at all.

Annie:
The word in the community is that he appropriates everyone else's ideas without acknowledging it was ever theirs first . . . I'm invisible again! Being invisible with him became too much for me.

She returns again to the idea of being invisible.

The session ends.

Discussion

Let's think about a short line of unconscious logic in this session.

The patient has talked about how in the beginning there is confusion and then a pattern emerges: both in art and in analysis. It can be a puzzle to figure things out – here again is the word 'figure', that played a prominent part in Monday's session. Then, with increased affect, she says that analysis offers a framework within which to think thoughts, and 'then you have the *patient*, and it becomes a whole different thing'. Note how in a matter of a few seconds she repeats the word 'whole': 'I was thinking about the process I've gone through here, from the beginning. The whole . . . metamorphosis.' Annie then proceeds to link this to the larva dream and insects.

We can see how in an earlier session she was thinking of a hole in the body – the cyst. This is to be removed some time later in the day, but other things have been removed – including her identity. The fact that Annie did not refer to her cyst operation in this session may be considered a form of unconscious thinking through enactment: to not mention that which had been on her mind – the removal of an object – constitutes an act of removal in itself.

Now there is the same sound but a different signifier: not a 'hole', but 'whole'. The word is immediately linked to metamorphosis and she says: 'I'm interested in what *word* you would use.' The wish to have a word for this new form of transformation, a word from the analyst, is an interesting wish and a different sort of action from those we have seen previously. It is not invasive; it searches for a new meaning. It occurs as she realises that the analytical process takes place within a frame. We would say that she discovers here the crucial difference between aloneness in the presence of the other,' which allows creative metamorphosis towards wholeness,' and isolation in a vacuum, which is a larval moment that leaves her existing as a hole.

So what word *would* we use? That is, how can we transform experience into speech? How can 'it' find a name?

The analyst says the field is rather dry of words for this and the patient says it is all very complex. This may be a way of stating that no word can speak this experience, especially this transformation, but the unconscious has already found many words, many similes and examples, that are transformative. To me, this part of the session feels deeper and more genuine – no longer glib and facile.

We may see from these sessions that free association can simultaneously express many unconscious ideas in many different ways. I have suggested that these various orders of expression are part of generically different forms of articulation that we may term 'categories of thought'.

I am maintaining that the analysand's unconscious does not lie. However, some are sceptical about this. Psychoanalysts frequently ask the question: what about the defences, or the resistances to free association?

Freud was clear that there were obvious resistances, such as silence or circumlocutionary verbosity. Certainly one cannot follow the analysand's free associations if he or she is silent, and it can equally be rather difficult to do if the analysand is overly verbose.

But we need to remember that free associating *is* unconscious thinking. In the process of revealing his or her thoughts it is obvious that the analysand will speak his or her defences. In Annie's case, for example, in the Monday session she is *seductive* (flirting with the analyst), she is *flippant* (joking about being asked for her licence), she *idealises* the object (her discourse on Marcus), she *identifies* with being an analyst over the weekend to protect herself against loss of the analyst, she *projectively identifies* her sense of diminishment – as a result of idealisation – into

Carlos, she *rationalises* important issues (telling Carlos this is all about his mother), and she is *reparative* (letting Carlos do the work on her studio) rather than contrite. Each of these actions is defensive. Each action protects her, in the moment, from some form of mental pain.

It is important, however, that we realise *who* is informing us of these defences. It is of course Annie herself. She is telling us who she is and how she functions. And she does so unconsciously, in the ordinary course of free association.

So while free associations do reveal logical processes of thought derived from the sequence of ideas, those thoughts will include defences against mental pain, as well as wishes, memories and relational expectations.

Indeed, one of the reasons for presenting Annie to the reader is that these sessions are saturated in her transference relationship. It would have been easy enough for the analyst, from the beginning of the Monday session, to focus entirely on her transference relation to him, and many analysts would probably have done just this. As we have seen, however, his decision was to allow her to talk on, unimpeded. He was well aware of the transference allusions to himself, but he was also alert to the fact that she was raising important questions from her unconscious that initiated valuable lines of thought. These thoughts, also concerning matters *outside* the transference, would never have been articulated by Annie had the analyst converted her discourse into references to himself.

We need to make a distinction between *working within* the transference and *interpreting* the transference. French and British psychoanalysts differ on this point. Listening to French sessions, British analysts often wonder: 'But why aren't they interpreting the transference?' The French reply is that, although they do now and then make a transference interpretation, they generally prefer to observe and follow the transference and work within it, rather than interpreting it.

Annie's psychoanalyst was very much aware of her transferences to him. In case presentations, he was often confronted by colleagues who insisted that he should be 'taking up' the transference. At times he was persuaded to

So, no doubt, SES has "presented" me, under some name, many, many times —

do this, but it always left him feeling that he was stealing a function that should have been Annie's own. He felt that she knew of this transference, that she used him for imaginatively romantic purposes, and although at times she would become manic with excitation he allowed her feelings to develop and listened to them calmly rather than interpreting what she was 'doing to him'.

or ?
coldness

This clinical stance demonstrates a remarkable respect for the analysand. It trusts that her enactments are forms of communication and that she is telling the analyst something, but not something about the transference alone. The patient is then free to use the transference to tell them both about all kinds of other features of her mental life and her past.

Looking back on these three sessions we might conclude that the transference allows Annie to hold on to the other without having to be cruel in order to guarantee the attachment. Although she reproaches the psychoanalyst for keeping a potential patient waiting, as he went ten minutes over time, she balanced that thought with the unconscious confession that 'it was nice', derived from the free association to her students who 'wanted to stay past 10 p.m. editing'. Implicit in this line of thought is Annie's experience and appreciation of the analyst's desire.

When Annie asks about 'the process I've gone through here' she adds, 'the whole . . . metamorphosis'. It is from this idea that she refers back to her dreams of being a larva and moving to 'fully functioning insect'.

The question arrives after the session in which the session overran, and she believes the analyst did this out of desire. But this is not a sexualised state of mind; it is the desire to be in the presence of the other, just as her students enjoyed being with her. Recalling the lesson of the educational requirements for Tess (just let her do her own thing, do not tell her what to do, give her time) and of Tess's story of the relation to her own grandfather (who had plenty of time for her), Annie answers the question she poses. She has changed because the analyst, although at times an object of erotic desire and of aggression, hate, and so forth, is an other who has provided her with a grandfatherly space in which she could go through the stages from crawling (like a caterpillar), back to a regressed progression (a larva looked after by the other), and eventually emerging as a flying self.

In answering her own question, Annie also solves a riddle that she poses when she says, 'Experience may be different between people, so you actually can make films that are *yours* – personal.' We puzzled here over the word 'may'. Recalling her fear of being invaded by the mother, we can assume that she 'spaced out' when so invaded. She nonetheless needed a reflective image from the other who would mirror her, but it could not be the mother. Who would it have to be?

It would have to be the self. Thus we can make more sense of the image of herself in the mirror and her conviction that the image moved. If one has to be an other to oneself – but different enough to make this split a useful one for personal growth – then self and image cannot be the same. The image in the mirror – standing in for the self – has to be separate.

Analysis, however, has allowed her to regress through the transference to a non-narcissistic solution, and therefore the need to find her own mirror image as a replacement for otherness. Annie can linger within the field of transference love, move back into a larval stage and then, through the passage of time, she can metamorphose into a new being.

Within her metaphor this new being is, of course, an 'insect' and we may wonder about quite *who or what* the analysis has created. Viewed as an object, within the field of object relations, then the image of a flying insect may evoke an image of flight, of mania, and so forth. Is she still on the path of a kind of manic transformation? This may be true to some extent; so too is the history of transformations that will have made such flight possible. As such, it seems to me to be a generative flight: a movement towards liberation.

Annie has discovered this within the transference. However exciting it might be to get into the analyst's mind and find shit in him, the need for this other, who helps her to grow and with whom she feels safe, is more fulfilling than the excitation of the moment.

We have by no means exhausted the numerous lines of thought within this hour, nor the links to Monday. Annie's sessions, however, do convey something of the thick complexity of unconscious articulation in a psychoanalysis.

10

Unconscious work

Psychoanalysis is a working partnership in which both analyst and patient have specific tasks. The fundamental aim of the analytical couple is to facilitate the expression of unconscious thinking, so that whatever ails the analysand – be it a symptom, a character trait, a disturbing mood, a relational ineptitude – the analysand and the psychoanalyst are provided with lots of information. Given enough information *from the unconscious*, most psychoanalysts will be in a position to help analysands discover those patterns of thought or behaviour that cause mental pain.

We have read Freud's recommendation that the analysand must say everything that crosses his or her mind. In fact, of course, no one can do that. Patients may find themselves silent for stretches of time because they are lost in thought or in the midst of evolving emotional experience. It would be counterproductive to demand that they interrupt such inner processes to report their thoughts to the analyst. Indeed, if the ideas crossing the mind are too embarrassing or disturbing, no analysand will elect to recount them. Although it is in the patient's interests to say as much as he or she can, fortunately psychoanalysis is not dependent on extracting such hidden thoughts from the nooks and crannies of the analysand's mind.

If I were to address the prospective analysand this is what I might say.

If the good news is that your analyst does not require you to tell him or her your darkest secrets, the bad news is that you are expected to talk to your analyst, to fulfil the duty to speak in detail about *many* of the events that cross your mind. Although no one can say *all* that is in the mind – indeed, that would amount to a form of obsessional symptomatology – you are expected to be *specific*. If you are telling the analyst about the events of the weekend it is constructive to describe in detail what took place. Instead of stating, 'I was with a friend on Friday night and we went out', it is more helpful to mention the name of the friend and to describe exactly where you went and what you did.

Why?

By describing seemingly unimportant events in detail you release yourself to speak from your unconscious. Unconscious thinking in an analysis operates through your ability to free yourself up to tell the analyst what you did, with whom, when, and what you thought and felt. When describing thoughts or feelings it is best to take your time and to be as precise as possible. It is non-cooperative to say simply, 'I felt fed up', rather than describing why you felt badly and over what, where you were, what was said and what you thought. It not only fails to give your analyst enough specific information to help him or her to understand you; it actually shuts down your own unconscious participation.

Understandably, most newcomers to psychoanalysis are sceptical about the value of being quite so detailed. What's in the name of a friend? Why give the title of the film you saw, rather than simply mentioning that you went to the cinema? Why describe the precise debate you had with a colleague, rather than simply saying you disagreed?

The answer is complex.

By being specific you not only provide the analyst with more information and open yourself to unconscious thinking, you actually *create* the session. By giving shape to the session through the provision of details, you unknowingly furnish it with many patterns, each of which constitutes a line of thought. Your psychoanalyst has developed what is an ordinary human ability to follow patterns into a particular form of art. He or she has been trained to listen in a state of deep concentration that will be guided by your creativity.

bore the PA

If this is creativity, what hope for true creativity—art?

If you want the analysis to be about you – specifically *you* – then you have to overcome the temptation to speak in clichés, lest your analyst's comments and view of you be likewise cliché-ridden.

If you are stuck at the beginning of a session about what to say – and this is quite common – then you should allow some minutes to pass. Most of the time something will pop into your mind. It may very well be a seemingly trivial detail: you suddenly recall seeing a television commercial about Palmolive soap and for some strange reason it irritated you. You might think this is too idiotic to report to someone like a psychoanalyst. The thought flashing into your mind will seem irrelevant, because you cannot make sense of it. But that is the point. It will have arrived out of a potential space that we might think of as the *possibility of the unconscious*, because it is the starting point for following a line of thought that will be driven by unconscious thinking.

As you are describing the annoying advert, something else – often seemingly unrelated – may occur to you. It is likely to be as apparently innocuous as the commercial. You might think next of a television series – maybe a specific episode of *The Simpsons* that you found amusing. One thought will lead to another, each arriving unbidden, and your task is simply to remain committed to speaking about what is crossing your mind. It may well be that these two brief associations – a Palmolive soap commercial and *The Simpsons* – link through the word 'soap': one a commercial for soap, the other an animated soap opera. It may be that the word 'palm' in 'Palmolive' links to a moment in *The Simpsons* when Homer threw his palms up in the air in exasperation.

The point is that by speaking *from the ordinary* you make unconscious expression possible. Such simple articulation alerts the analyst's unconscious to tune in to your wavelength. It may be that nothing of note will happen for quite some time. But the more you speak, the more lines you create, the more your unconscious is establishing those particular issues that are preoccupying you in the analysis.

Enough said to the imaginary patient.

To speak from the ordinary proves one is nobody – a nonentity.

Let us consider the resistances to free association.

The clearest resistance is wilful silence. If the patient *will* not talk – and of course there can be many reasons for this – then the analytical process will be slowed up considerably. Even though such silence may be informative in some respects, either within the transference or as evidence of the arrival of deeply upsetting thoughts, the core of an analysis depends on the analysand's free talking.

The most common defence against free association, however, is what we might think of as 'rambling abstraction'. It is best to give an example.

Hi. I hope you had a good weekend. Mine was, well, really rather a bit of a loss. I mean, I met up with some friends and we did a few things but nothing really. Then I got anxious. You know, just general worries – the usual stuff. And I acted out. I went out, had too much to eat, and probably gained a few pounds. Then a sleepless night on . . . was it Friday? I think Friday. Could have been Saturday. At times like these I think of what you said once to me, that I can get down on myself and, like, this getting down on myself is not helpful. And I am sure you're right. So . . . I think it was Sunday . . . I did a good thing. I went out and did some things that made me feel better. You know, all that stuff in my childhood, well, I just have to try and put that aside as I can get caught up in it. So, I'm really glad to be here because I really needed to tell you this stuff.

Now let's imagine an intervention – one that many psychoanalysts might find themselves making rather routinely: 'I think you missed me and were a bit at a loss until now.'

The analysand has, in effect, said nothing. Saying nothing is not necessarily insignificant – the production of nothing could be a matter of interest to the psychoanalyst and it could be serving many purposes. For the most part, however, the patient's report on the weekend is a resistance.

We do not know why the weekend was 'a loss'. We do not know which friends the patient met up with, or what they did. Therefore we do not know why he was anxious. We do not know what is meant by 'the usual stuff'. The patient's cure – overeating – is a self-interpretation that we are meant to accept as an explanation for his state, but then his failure to recall which night he was sleepless seems offhand. His use of a prior interpretation by the analyst to somehow bolster his account is as empty as his discourse and, of course, we do not know what 'stuff' from his childhood he is thinking about.

Before we can determine the nature of the patient's unconscious resistance we should first ask ourselves whether the analyst has colluded in the creation of an empty discourse. By failing to elicit more detail, has the analyst actually endorsed an impoverished narrative and settled for an absence of unconscious communication?

How might the analyst have responded differently to the rather empty account offered by the patient? One alternative approach would be to *echo* certain words or phrases. The echo would be delivered in a way that indicated the analyst's wish for more detail. 'Your weekend was a bit of a loss?' 'You met up with friends?' 'You did a few things?' These are all questions that repeat the patient's wording. If the analysand answers these queries with a more detailed description then something interesting generally happens. From this point on, the patient will continue to speak to the analyst in much greater detail.

What do we learn from this?

We learn, amongst other things, that contemporary analysands tend not to believe that their analysts are genuinely interested in the particles of their lives. From the first interpretation mentioned above, the patient will receive the unconscious message that the analyst is empty of genuine therapeutic curiosity and is content to bide his or her time listening to platitudes. If the analyst accepts nothing – an absence of real communication – then it is easy enough for this patient to conclude that the analyst sees him as someone for whom the production of nothing is normal.

As nothing will come of nothing, why would a patient stay in this form of treatment? The answer is troubling.

Analysands who receive nothing but a kind of passive empathic response may conclude that, since they are in fact rather hopeless, they are fortunate to have found a benign figure to look after them. A vicious circle is established. The patient assumes that in accepting the production of nothing, the analyst is implying that the patient amounts to nothing. For many an analysand this is an uncanny reproduction of a childhood situation in which parents transcended the specific terms of their child's character and identity. This child runs home eager to tell his mother about something that has just happened out in the street. Without waiting for him to finish his story the mother says, 'Oh, how nice, dear', as if this seemingly empathic comment actually receives the communication. The child's conclusion is that he is not worthy of true interest; such a comment displaces unconscious reception with empathic phatic formula.

Another kind of patient, however, might accomplish a similar resistance but in a different and more sophisticated way.

Patient: I spent quite a lot of time this weekend thinking about what you said, or implied, last session. As I understood it, you were making the point that I do not believe in my way of life and because of this loss of belief, which has eluded me but permeated me, there is thus a kind of – I think you called it 'psychic sink-hole' – into which I fall, but because I do not see it, I fall without knowing it. In fact, I recall your saying that when I feel 'grounded' this is only because actually I am falling in a sink-hole but think I am grounded because I still see the earth, but am actually falling fast. I have given this a lot of thought. I agree that I do not believe in my life and that I am drawn to vacuums. No. To vacuousness. But I wonder if this thinking is my way of being a transparent self. Might I be just sort of opening myself up to something that has to sink me? I have felt for some weeks in here this feeling of sinking, of sinking into something. I feel it is a sort of disappearing into something inexorable. Something hard to put into words.

Something that is drawing me, pulling me. A force. A force that has a kind of feel to it like something not me, not human, but something calling me. I wonder now if this force could be used to get me up and out of the vacuum? I can feel, in saying this, a sort of lighter self, a lighter being. I feel . . . I feel silent now.

Analyst: Perhaps you have allowed yourself to sink without use of a hole, but finding a whole for yourself.

This analytic pair might appear at first sight to be engaged in some rather deep philosophical analysis. Heavy signifiers like 'belief' are used with considerable frequency *as if* analyst and analysand are engaged in a profound meeting of minds. Bion may be invoked by analysts inclined toward this way of working, and their sessions bear a striking similarity to Beckett's plays.

These two imaginary clinical examples might seem to be very different, but in fact both analytic pairs are engaged in empty, non-productive discourse. It would be difficult to determine who is creating these analysands' production of −K. However, sadly enough, I find it is often the analyst who is the more responsible party.

What reasons are given for this kind of folly?

Arlene's analyst recognised early on in the session that her material – the analyst's phone did not pick up; the president of the Conservatory did not listen; people expect her to do all the talking; the long silence which followed – could be understood within the transference. Yet the analyst did not translate these comments into a transference interpretation. Why not?

The analyst reported that she felt that these thoughts were part of a more extensive thought process, the understanding of which should not be limited to the transference. When I asked the analyst if she could describe why she felt this way, she replied that she could sense a certain momentum of thought within her patient, a momentum guided by feelings which were on their way but which had not yet arrived. Even when Arlene fell silent for three minutes or so, the analyst felt that her analysand was engaged in analytical work.

As we know, the analyst's feelings proved to be essential to the arrival in the session of a profound insight by Arlene that answered a convergence of many questions: 'Why do I persist?', 'Why do I have to be the one to talk?', 'Why if I say something once do I feel I do not have to say it again?' and so on. Yet at the time of her 'uninterpretation' – to quote Winnicott's theory of the uninterpretive function of the analyst – the analyst knew only that she should simply allow her patient to go on thinking. This was based entirely on a feeling.

We may ask: what is this feeling?

I would say that all but the psychotic personality know it. It is based on the self's intuition in listening to the other – even if the other is stumbling about in speech, or silent, or momentarily focusing on some acute issue – that the other is heading towards something that has not yet arrived. So we are silent or, if we speak, we try not to focus the analysand's attention on one thing or another. By simply attending and following the line of associations, we facilitate the process of thought.

This sense derives from the self's unconscious perception of the other's unconscious workings. We may not know consciously where the other's thoughts are heading, yet there is an underlying feeling that this is logical.

In *This is Your Brain on Music*, Daniel Levitin discusses how the brain makes calculated guesses about perceptions, referring to Helmholtz's theory of 'unconscious inference' and Irvin Rock's concept of 'the logic of perception'. One can look at this phenomenon from the perspective of neuropsychology or from the conceptual field of psychoanalysis, but it is not difficult to see that these two different ways of seeing the world converge around the phenomenon of unconscious perception. 'What we see and hear,' writes Levitin, 'is the end of a long chain of mental events that give rise to an impression, a mental image, of the physical world.'[36] How close this is to Freud's own concept of the work of evenly suspended attentiveness and the discovery of the chain of thoughts that reveals the pattern of the internal world.

It is clear that analysts listening to their patients' associations unconsciously search for patterns of all kinds.

That said, however, there are clearly times in a session when the psychoanalyst feels that something else is going on. The sense may be that the patient is emptying the self of meaning, evacuating it through language, affect, gesture or psycho-drama. This does not mean that narrative free association has ceased. The argument of this book is that, as they talk, people inevitably reveal chains of thought within their narrative. But if the analyst does not feel that unconscious work is taking place, this may indicate that the genesis of meaning (or resistance) may reside in another form.

Analysts describing their states of mind at moments like this will commonly say that they stopped listening to the material in evenly suspended attentiveness and asked themselves what was happening. As the analysand's associations will inevitably have been in part transferential, the analyst may then see that the feeling of interruption to the unconscious work has to do with issues in the transference, or it may be that the flow of associations has been influenced by certain affective arrests, or ego defences.

Of course, these moments carry their own meaning, but they will be exceptions to the work of unconscious thinking achieved through the process of free association. Whatever transpires, if the analyst has an open mind, he or she will follow the drift of the session, shifting listening positions depending on the determinations of the analysand's unconscious.

The sessions we have reviewed in Chapters 7–9 raise far more questions than we can answer.

One of the findings from the micro-analysis of clinical material is that unconscious thinking poses seemingly incessant questions which set in motion sequences of answers, which in turn spawn further questions. Indeed, it would seem that we are endlessly curious about why we think what we do. Our thoughts and feelings are constantly raising questions, which we proceed to work on, most of the time outside of consciousness.

Looked at this way, the dreamer is by day a questioner. Lived experiences evoke associations of all kinds – memories, desires, anxieties, axioms – that combine into a series of questions. Caroline behaves badly in the presence of a conference secretary. That night she has a dream about not having any food in the fridge. Her dream poses a question: *why* does she not have enough to feed her boyfriend? Her associations answer, almost immediately, that it is because she prefers to be the one who is looked after. That line of thought also partly answers the question of her childish behaviour in the presence of the conference secretary: everyone should look after her. But this childlike state of mind impresses her between sessions and she arrives with a new question: why does she behave like this? As we discovered, this question leads back to her relationship with an aunt whom she idealised but also loved so intensely that she rather lost her own sense of identity.

So a simple event in Caroline's day – an impetuous response to a conference secretary – evokes associations during that day, and in the night she has a dream which ties together many of the threads elicited by her lived experience. What we witness is an oscillating process in which questions produce answers that then raise new questions. We can see, indeed, a relationship between unconscious and conscious thinking. A question posed by the unconscious strikes consciousness: why did I have this dream? Caroline does not know, but she free associates and her unconscious proceeds to answer, at least in part.

But how conscious is Caroline of what is on her mind? She remembers the dream, she thinks about Edward, who provides for her, she mulls over her strange behaviour with the conference secretary, and she recalls life with her aunt. So a lot crosses her mind consciously. What she cannot see, of course, are the links between these disparate ideas – at least, not as they occur. In other words, like the rest of us, she cannot witness the actual work of unconscious thinking.

This should not be so surprising, after all. Most of our perceptions during the day, what they bring to mind, how they affect our moods and the dreams which follow: these are not conscious. The occasional piece of thought-content crosses the mind, but its place in our matrix of thinking is not clear to us.

What is unconscious work? It is *a form* of thinking that is ⸺
outside consciousness. Since infancy – well before the
arrival of meaningful states of consciousness – we have been
processing information. That information arrives from two
sources: the external environment and our internal world.
For every event in the real we experience internal events
produced from our drives, our anxieties, and so forth. The
two worlds intersect in our ego, which arranges the two sets
of impressions and organises them into primitive storage
areas that begin to constitute our unconscious knowledge. At
the same time, however, our ego (the term Freud used
sometimes, but not always, for the organisation of all unconscious activity) develops increased capacities for perceiving
our world, for sorting our perceptions, for creating dreams,
daydreams, talking points, and all the stuff of human life.

In the clinical examples of Arlene, Caroline and Annie
we are fortunate to witness a small sample of unconscious
work. And the evidence in these sessions, and in every
analytic hour, reveals how the analysand develops unconscious insight into the self.   *develops for what?*

You will recall Annie's musings on her love of her   *for*
analyst. From there she discusses her new relationship   *whom?*
with Marcus, whom she believes she puts on a pedestal.   *where?*
She tells a friend, Carlos, about Marcus, and as Carlos is
subjected to Annie's comparison of him with Marcus he
feels diminished. Time passes. The next day Annie makes
reparation to Carlos by encouraging his creative activity in
her studio. Later she is able to state that she knows she
diminishes people and takes pleasure in these forms of
cruelty. She then concludes that Tess, her student, needs
Annie's affirmation, not her criticism. The insight? Instead
of diminishing the other, one must celebrate the other's
creativity. Although the presence of the analyst is crucial to
Annie's unconscious work, we can see nonetheless that she
develops her insights herself, without interpretive intervention.

Many schools of analytical thought would argue that
the mutative moments in psychoanalysis can be brought
about only through analytical interpretation. Unquestion-
ably, especially in the deconstruction of a symptom or a

character disorder, interpretation is very important. Yet it is not to diminish its role to point out that the evidence provided by these sessions – and scores of others – indicates that most analytical work and insight is actually accomplished through unconscious thinking.

When Arlene works her way from wondering about whether she has persisted long enough in calling her psychoanalyst to discovering that she did in fact persist in reaching her father, against her mother's wishes, she comes to a very moving moment in her life history. Along the way she has wondered why she has found it hard to speak more than once, why she could not speak to her deaf cousin, and why her only vivid memory of time spent with her mother is of being read a passage in Greek. These and other ideas cross her mind and reveal many different lines of thought, but one theme beats like a drum through this session: do I persist, or do I give up? Which of the two beings is she? She comes to recognise that, although one part of her is terrified of maternal anger or abandonment, she has persisted in overcoming her anxieties to fulfil some of her wishes in the present and in the past. Arlene *realises* that her truth is, ultimately, that she is someone who does persist.

Such realisations are profound moments in the life of an analysand. They are moments in which people discover something new in the course of its arrival from the unconscious. These are, then, emotional moments. Although they may have made use of the verbal assistance of the analyst, they can occur entirely through the self's own free-associative journey in an hour.

We may say, following Bion, that analysands have preconceptual knowledge of the fundamental issues that occupy the self. Their questions, then, are essential to the destiny of the preconceived. Through unconsciously asking questions, the self is in search of an emotional answer that realises the preconception and gives a profound sense of inner meaning. It is important to understand that such a realisation may take place purely unconsciously. But if we think about this, it makes sense. How many times during our lives, whether perhaps reading a novel, walking in the woods, talking to a friend or listening to a certain piece of music, do we have some epiphanic registration? Are there not thousands of times when we feel that something which is just now taking place is deeply meaningful? We cannot articulate why it is so important; indeed, it is meaningful precisely *because* we do not understand why.

Such experiences do often lead to a conceptualisation – 'I really loved that piece of music'; 'that was a great conversation with Gerald' – but not necessarily one that enters consciousness in the form of an insight into the self or life. These conscious realisations are important – Caroline works out that she seeks dependent relations in order to disappear into the protective custody of an aunt, but that this also deprives her of a sense of her own identity. But we are engaged in thousands of evolving interests, and this network is far too complex to allow more than a tiny proportion of our unconscious trains of thought to come into consciousness.

However, we do not ordinarily succumb to despair or pessimism about the limits of our knowledge. Even these partial realisations contribute to a *sense of meaning* in our lives. The people we know, the cultural objects we encounter, the places we visit, our accidental discoveries, our dreams, the 'stuff' of living: we feel that all this is nourishing. We feel that as time passes we are gaining wisdom, even if we do not know what that is or how to conjure it.

Much of the work of a psychoanalysis – from the analyst's point of view – consists of interpreting patterns in the patient's mental life and behaviour. Even though an analysand might continually present the same pathological structure (a disturbed pattern of being and relating), the way it shows up in the material – in descriptions of events in the real, in the patient's emotional state, via the transference, and so forth – means that there is endless variation in character presentation. The analyst will hear the same thing in many different ways. He or she will interpret the same structure according to the form of its delivery, and the analyst's unconscious choice of wording for an interpretation will a highlight a particular facet of the problem in that moment.

For example, I can think of one analysand who presented to his analyst essentially the same character
problem for nearly five years. In one form or another each
session re-presented it. At the core, he lived in a state of
perpetual frustration because the world of reality did not
correspond to the world of his fantasies. Each day he
expected people to fulfil his wishes and when they did not
he always responded in the same way. He would retreat
into a silent and sullen mood that varied in intensity
depending on the person he was with, but his long-suffering
wife bore the brunt of the most intense sulks. He was
forever leaving the room to go and hide somewhere in his
vast house. She was forever trying to find him, he would
pretend that he did not hear her, and she would end up a
nervous wreck. At other times he would retreat by providing insufficient information to others so they were kept
in the dark about what he was thinking and feeling. In
effect, the world did not deserve to hear from him. His
anger, at times, was so intense that he would suffer disturbing physical symptoms and had been treated for a
heart condition. All this behaviour entered the transference. He treated his analyst with contempt, offset with
bouts of idealised praise, in order to feed-by-his-demand an
ideal other who was meant to provide him with what he
wanted. In one form or another he was perpetually angry
with the analyst, but invariably innocent of this anger.

The persistence of this pathology could have engen-
dered a psychoanalytic situation in which interpretations
became 'closed'. The analyst had to be careful not to labour
her interpretations too much, lest the analysand feel that
he was the object of an endlessly repeated statement. She
had to work with this character pattern almost as if, each
time, it was something new. In this way the variations in
the presentation allowed the analyst's idiom to operate in a
realm of freedom that could otherwise have become
foreclosed by the incarcerating pattern of the analysand's
character disorder.

This kind of work occupies many psychoanalyses, and
many analysands present such complex and diverse character patterns that they can only be comprehended over a

considerable length of time. These patients pose a question – 'Why am I like this?' – and week after week, month after month, new material arrives that in some form or another provides new clues.

To take another example, one analysand stated during the first year of analysis that she was sure she would not have been a good mother. She worked in a horticultural nursery where she tended to her plants, and she and her husband had two dogs, three cats, fish, and other animals which they looked after passionately. The analyst had a feeling early on that the patient's idea that she would not be a good mother was simply wrong, and he said so. In evidence for his conviction the analyst said that she was a nurturing woman and the maternal instinct was evident in her choice of profession and the way she lived her life. Later, reflecting on the way she took great care to present the analyst with material *within* reverie, the analyst added that he felt she was tending to him with maternal care.

Nonetheless, the analysand did not believe these assurances and, we might ask, why should she? The analyst offered them not as interpretative understandings but as convictions that arrived out of his countertransference. He was impressed by the analysand's persistence in posing the question concerning her belief about motherhood, something that had been the source of a deep, near-suicidal depression when she was in her thirties.

Then in the sixth year of analysis the patient brought up this dilemma again, in passing, in a Monday session. The previous Friday she had discussed how her rather fearsome father, no longer alive, had been on her mind. On many occasions she had described how he had become a model for her throughout her childhood – he was the figure whom she admired most because he was a pillar of strength. On the Tuesday she turned her attention to her elderly mother. She began the hour stating that she was once again irritated by her mother's impulsiveness. The analyst asked for associations and this time her attention directed itself to how the mother was just giving away money to one of the patient's siblings. The session focused on how maternal impulsivity elicited rivalry in the patient

– indeed, in all the other siblings. The session ended with the analysand commenting that she hated being in this oldest-sister role, always having to correct her mother.

On Wednesday, recollecting aspects of the Tuesday session, the analysand said that she found her mother's voice of disapproval so depressing. Her affect thickened during the hour and she became depressed. She felt that her mother's failure to self-regulate forced her into being the kind of person that she did not want to be. Self-critically, however, the patient added that she knew she had contempt for her mother and she wondered if she was simply looking for reasons to blame her. The analyst asked if this was really so, given that the mother's impulsivity had set the siblings into competition with one another, and the analysand's anger returned. She withdrew her last comment, saying she thought it was a rationalisation and that she was avoiding something.

After the session the analyst reported feeling that between the two of them something new was happening. There was an urgency to the session – but also there was something different. It was quite simple: the patient had made the crucial link between maternal impulse and sibling rivalry. During the next session the patient turned her attention back to her father and the analyst said, in passing, 'I suppose if your father were still alive your mother would not be in charge of the money and the disturbance with the siblings would not be so active.' This made immediate sense to the analysand. She said, 'It is awful to have to be the father.'

And out of the blue the analyst found himself saying, 'You cannot be a good mother if you are the father.'

Who knows *why* this simple comment, at this moment in the analysis, became a transformational event for the analysand and the psychoanalyst? The analyst was as moved by this truth as the patient was. It was as if something so obvious, that had been staring them in the face over the years, had now become clear.

In fact the main ideas of the week had all been mentioned previously. Years before, following a dream, the patient had said that she felt so identified with her father that she did not feel like a woman. This led to feelings that she had been a 'tomboy' and to her ambivalence about being a woman. It also led her to say that this was, at least in part, why she felt she was not destined to be a mother.

So what was different about the week described above?

Of course, we shall never know for sure. But it was something about the way matters were organised unconsciously *this* time that brought all the crucial elements (contents and affects) together, so that analyst and analysand could work as an unconscious unit with a high degree of creativity. The analyst reported that his interpretation felt to him to be an inspired one: it just popped right out. It was not a particularly new idea, but it was now living in a new milieu: it had taken on a fresh significance in the context of the analysand's free-associative organisations and in turn it constituted a realisation between analyst and patient.

Such inspired interpretations in analysis are not frequent. But when they do occur they are evidence of a profound change taking place in the analysand.

As we have seen, Freud's classical method relies upon the practice of evenly suspended attentiveness. Given the task – to catch the drift of the patient's unconscious with the analyst's own unconscious – it is understandable that the classical analytical position is one in which the analyst does not say much. He or she is listening in a very particular sort of way. But does Freud believe that the analyst will eventually be able to discover 'forgotten material' – that there is something specific which the analyst is looking for, and will find, if he or she listens in this manner? Certainly now and then the analyst will discover something forbidden, something repressed, but Freud's theory of the density of unconscious processes, embedded in his theory of intersecting lines of thought, means that no one session could ever be focused on the retrieval of one or more particular repressed ideas.

There will be points of convergence, and at times these will bring the discovery of forgotten material that may elucidate the structure of a symptom or help to unravel the meaning of a dream. But what about the rest? What about all those lines of thought that do not result in analytical interpretation? This theory of unconscious thinking and unconscious articulation suggests that it would be quite impossible for the analyst to gather up all the threads of what the patient is presenting in a session.

Time and again, when supervising cases, it strikes me that both the analyst and the analysand are hard at work on something without either of them knowing what that 'something' is. Indeed, the more deeply involved an analyst is in the analytical process, the less likely he or she is to know consciously what is taking place. The analyst must be lost in a form of reverie that is designed not for conscious consideration of what is transpiring, but for enabling unconscious work.

Presenting a case to a group of colleagues can be a hazardous enterprise for the psychoanalyst who is working in this way. In the competitive atmosphere of such situations analysts tend not to sit back and listen freely. Instead they adopt a position of selective listening. They look out for their favourite object of theoretical desire – be it the castration complex, the transference, the dissociated state – that will naturally organise the material and prejudice what is heard.

Selective listening is antithetical to the position of evenly suspended attentiveness proposed by Freud, but all analysts will inevitably succumb to it at times, whether driven by ideological mandate or by their acquired knowledge of the patient. It is hard sometimes to listen afresh.

At moments like this it is best to remind ourselves of the fundamental nature of free association. Whatever the analyst has learned from the patient in the past, whatever themes have already been illuminated, all patients propose new questions. What one has learned will inevitably be displaced by new thoughts crossing the mind or themes hinted at before, perhaps, but never previously foregrounded.

It seems that an analysand will persist in posing a question if it remains unanswered by either of the two participants. Once it has been 'seen', usually unconsciously and occasionally consciously, it recedes and gives way to new questions. Over time one can begin to discern this *free-associative momentum*. One senses that the patient is working on issues and, although some of these works will arrive in consciousness and are discussable, to stop the analysand at such a moment is to interrupt a work in progress – rather like interrupting the writing of a poem.

When unconscious thinking is taking place, one must allow one's own unconscious receptivity to engage with the analysand's unconscious work. This will take place through silent listening," in occasional echoes, or sometimes in seemingly offbeat, spontaneous comments that have little apparent connection to what the analysand is talking about. Sometimes these will seem innocuous. Annie's psychoanalyst says that she seems to feel freer speaking to him. Why did he say that? Considering this later, he reported that he had no idea. In fact he was reflecting the word 'say' which Annie was hard at work thinking about, but it is important that he did *not* know why he said it. This 'not knowing' is the   ?
foundation for the capacity to work at the level of unconscious creativity.

Of course, we must be aware of a potential danger in this perspective. It can turn into a rationale for 'just being' with the analysand, or for 'resonating with her experience'. How are we to judge between these two frames of mind: between the analyst who is engaged in reverie which facilitates unconscious communication, and the one who is 'out to lunch' and just wasting time?

While it is possible that neither would be able to answer the question 'What do you think is going on?', the disciplined analyst" will be able to describe in detail what the patient has been talking about. And we can find additional evidence in the quality of the patient's responses. The psychoanalyst who is engaged in unconscious commu-   ??
nication" with the analysand is a highly productive participant in this process, and his or her patient will generally respond to the analyst's comments with a flow of associative material. Although the analysand may not be aware of 'where this is all going', he or she will nonetheless talk on –   No
reporting details from the previous day, remembering events in the recent past, recalling daydreams, and so forth

B. assumes the UCS is "creative" – but to what end?

– without anxiety about what this will add up to. Neither participant will feel the need to come up with some kind of organising interpretation that they can take home with them after the hour.

The comments of the lazy or undisciplined analyst tend not to elicit further free associations from the patient. Later, although this analyst may be able to outline broad themes in the material, he or she will not recall the detail and sequence of the analysand's thoughts.

In short, it is possible to differentiate between good and bad technique. Whatever the analyst's theoretical background, if he or she listens and elicits free-associative material, then this is good analysis. If the analyst's work – however brilliant it may seem in the exercising of a theory – does not elicit spontaneous free association, then this is not good analysis. It is a matter of whether or not there is deep unconscious work taking place within and between the analytic pair.

11

The infinite question

Sophocles' *Oedipus the King* begins with a question. As the citizens of Thebes protest in front of the king's palace, Oedipus challenges their presence: 'Why do you sit here with your suppliant crowns?' He asks what they fear or want, and the priest replies that the plague on the city is the cause of their misery.[37]

Oedipus certainly knows why they are complaining. His question is rhetorical and allows him to reproach the citizens by stating that no one is in greater pain than himself, for he must suffer for all the citizens of Thebes. He reassures the crowd by telling them that he has sent Creon to the Pythian temple of Apollo to discover what might be done to save the city.

Creon returns with a curious message. A man must be banished from Thebes, for it is 'murder guilt' that sustains the curse on the city. Oedipus's response to Creon is of interest. There are thirteen rapid-fire exchanges between the two and then, when Creon states that he has an answer to the cause of the plague, Oedipus responds with questions: 'What is the rite of purification?' 'How shall it be done?' 'Who is this man whose fate the God pronounces?' In the course of fifty-six lines Oedipus asks no fewer than eleven questions, in twelve exchanges between Creon and himself. The *force* of such questioning creates a powerful sense of momentum. One feels that Oedipus will stop at nothing until his questions are answered.

Towards the end of the play, however, we meet a very different Oedipus. At this point his questions seem strangely lacking in urgency; indeed, they indicate a notable lack of interest in knowing the identity of the murderer who has brought the plague. Again the conversation is between Creon and Oedipus. Oedipus blames Creon for summoning Tiresias, who has pointed to Oedipus as the murderer. Oedipus asks whether Creon did not urge Oedipus to send for Tiresias, and Creon says that he did, and will stand by what he has told Oedipus. Oedipus's reply comes out of the blue: 'How long ago is it since Laius . . .' At which point, Creon breaks in with a question of his own: 'What about Laius? I don't understand.' In other words, Creon cannot understand the free association.

Continuing to talk to Creon, Oedipus again peppers the dialogue with question after question. Did Laius vanish, or was he murdered? Was Tiresias then known as a seer? Following the murder, did he point the finger at Oedipus? Did they search for the killer? Why didn't Tiresias say anything at the time?

The apparent urgency of these questions is striking because they come so late in the day. Indeed, in his earlier exchange with Creon, Oedipus displayed a remarkable lack of curiosity about Laius. Creon states that 'before you piloted the state we had a king called Laius' – to which Oedipus replies, 'I know of him by hearsay. I have not seen him.'

What is this about?

If Oedipus displays at this moment a myopia born of hubris, Jocasta's failure to tell Oedipus of a most worrying prophecy must be the dramatic exemplar of the Freudian slip: the power of the forgotten. Creon's conclusion is that Oedipus must be guilty of the murder of Laius, but Jocasta tells her son, 'Do not concern yourself about this matter.' She says she has a proof that he cannot be the murderer. Although an oracle had told Laius that his son would kill him, Jocasta says that he was killed by robbers (more than one) and, furthermore, that Laius had pierced his son's ankles and then abandoned him on a hillside.

Oedipus is now driven by questions that arise out of what he hears from Jocasta. She said Laius was killed at a crossroads: he wants to know how long ago, he wants to know what Laius looked like. The questions, again, are striking for not having been asked earlier, and now they have the force of the *après-coup*, of questions deferred that now carry a horror embedded in the very act of questioning.

But let us return to Jocasta. What are we to make of the fact that she has been sleeping with Oedipus for all these years and seems not to have thought about his wounded feet? Following the murder of her husband, one would have thought the prophecy might have occurred to her; and if this did cross her mind, why she did not ask questions?

'O God, I think I have called curses on myself in ignorance,' says Oedipus – hitting the nail right on the head. Earlier, Tiresias has poured scorn on Oedipus for his ignorance of his situation: 'You know nothing,' he says. 'So, muddy with contempt my words and Creon's! Misery shall grind no man as it will you.'

For Freud, *Oedipus the King* exemplifies the unconscious nature of the complex to be named after Oedipus. The wish to kill the father and bed the mother is so powerful that it will be achieved in some form or another, even though the price paid by the child will be very high indeed. We may see how part of the success of this wish lies in the ignorance of its fulfilment, which can be accomplished only through conscious blindness. Freud argued that the epistemophilic drive posed the first conscious question to the subject: what is one to make of the sight of genital difference?

The play, however, is also a remarkable example of the power of questions driven by various forms of ignorance. Oedipus has solved the riddle posed by the Sphinx: 'What creature walks on four legs in the morning, two at noon, and three in the evening?' Since the Sphinx was holding Thebes in terror until this riddle was solved, Creon had promised his sister Jocasta in marriage to the man who could find the answer: 'Man walked on his hands and feet when he was young, at noon in middle life he walked erect, and in the afternoon of life he walked with the aid of a walking stick.'[38] When Oedipus solved this riddle the Sphinx was destroyed and the Thebans assumed that Oedipus had thereby saved the city.

The situation itself is a conundrum. How could the riddle be solved if Jocasta was already married, given that Creon had promised that the one who solved the riddle could wed her? The answer must be that Jocasta, through fate or fortune, must be a free woman. In other words, Laius would have to be murdered in order for the solver of the riddle to gain his prize. The murder of Laius is thus a precondition for the solution to the plague.

Sophocles shows us that one may solve one question, but no matter how finite it may seem, the answer will be displaced by latent questions embedded within it. We live, then, within the drive of an infinite question.

However much we believe we are solving our problems, each solution brings new questions that undermine certainty. Sophocles makes it clear that we shall suffer this fact as a condition of our existence; it is not only thematically stated in the drama, it is part of its structure. The most famous slip in the play occurs when the Chorus and Oedipus are discussing the murder of Laius. 'It was said that he was killed by certain wayfarers,' observes the Chorus, to which Oedipus replies, 'I heard that, too, but no one saw the killer.' Here Sophocles allows us to see the way Oedipus's unconscious knowledge corrects the Chorus: it was not several people who killed Laius, it was one.

Let us now jump forward some two thousand years to Shakespeare, and Freud's other favourite play. Like *Oedipus the King*, *Hamlet* also pivots around the murder of a father and a king. The murder of Hamlet's father, however, is no distant or forgotten murder: it is so fresh in people's minds that at the beginning of the play the guards see the ghost of the dead king.

Both plays also start with a question. At the beginning of *Hamlet*, Barnardo asks, 'Who's there?'[39] A deceptively simple question, for sure. It would seem to be prompted by the sight of the ghost. But when Hamlet is persuaded to come and look for himself, what does he see? Shakespeare gives us a conversation in which the ghost is embodied with a sharp clarity of memory and vision. 'Remember me' echoes in Hamlet's mind on their parting.

The ghost re-enters in Act III Scene 4, as Hamlet confronts his mother:

O Hamlet, speak no more:
Thou turn'st mine eyes into my very soul;
And there I see such black and grained spots
As will not leave their tinct.

Unlike the guards in the first scene, Gertrude does not see the ghost and presumes Hamlet to be mad:

Alas, how is't with you
That you do bend your eye on vacancy
And with the incorporal air do hold discourse?

Who's there?
The reappearance of the ghost reverses several events. It returns to prompt Hamlet to exact revenge:

Do not forget. This visitation
Is but to whet thy almost blunted purpose.

Until the arrival of the ghost, Hamlet's summary of his mother's actions has been lucid and effective but, ironically, the ghost's appearance gives Gertrude the upper hand as Hamlet now appears to have lost his mind. The apparition remains on stage but is mute as she undermines Hamlet with her questions:

Queen: To whom do you speak this?
Hamlet: Do you see nothing there?
Queen: Nothing at all; yet all that is I see.
Hamlet: Nor did you nothing hear?
Queen: No, nothing but ourselves.

At this point the ghost departs and Hamlet points after him – 'Look, where he goes, even now, out at the portal' – and his mother concludes that he is hallucinating: 'This is the very coinage of your brain.'
Who's there?
If, along with Hamlet, we have seen a convincing ghost in the first scene, this second appearance is intended to

raise doubts. Hamlet's psychic revenge on the mother, by getting her to look into her soul, is impeded by his appearance of madness, but it also raises in the audience's mind a question about whether the ghost ever was truly visible to anyone except Hamlet.

This question, over the appearance of presence or the presence of nothing, earlier raises a question about being itself. 'To be or not to be, that is the question,' says Hamlet, in the first words of the world's most famous speech. Why, he asks, must man suffer so – 'When he himself might his quietus make/With a bare bodkin?'

Martin Heidegger, arguably the greatest philosopher of the twentieth century, begins *An Introduction to Metaphysics* with a question: 'Why is there being rather than nothingness?' In *The Myth of Sisyphus*, Albert Camus – probably the most popular philosopher across the generations of that century – argues that there is only one thought we must confront. It is a question: Why not commit suicide?

'Who's there?' is a question posed about who we are, where we are, why we are here, what we are to make of our being, and how we are to face our ending.

Sophocles and Shakespeare give us two plays about the murder of a father–king and of sexual transgressions with the widowed mother, all to end in a swathe of violence that calls into question the sanity of being human. These are plays that seem driven by question piling upon question piling upon question.

Even though the characters in the plays seem to develop answers, no sooner do they think they know something than new questions enter the scene, to dispel the respite of certainty.

Freud wrote of an epistemophilic drive, a drive to know. He sometimes linked it to the scopophilic drive: the wish to look. 'To look' and 'to look into' have an affinity.

Although Freud examined this drive in the context of the child's curiosity about sexual difference, I think it is more accurate to state that the force of questioning resides in the pressure brought to bear on the mind to think unthought knowledge.

In *Oedipus the King* the Sphinx creates a riddle that asks, in effect, whether man can identify himself. Instinctively Oedipus comes up with the answer. Knowledge will drive the question. Until then, however, the people of Thebes have been numbed by the terrifying presence of the riddle-making monster. Like the Stepford Wives, the Thebans seem markedly lacking in basic curiosity. The one who poses questions is a grotesque figure: 'A terrible monster with the head and breasts of a woman, body of a dog, tail of a serpent, wings of a bird, paws of lion, and a human voice.'[40]

This seems to be an example of extractive introjection – a psychological act in which one person removes a function from the other (or others).[41] The Sphinx has taken into herself the function of curiosity, leaving the citizens of Thebes blind, ignorant and unable to wonder. All except Tiresias, who seems almost like her offspring. According to one myth, Tiresias became blind because he saw two snakes mating, killed the female and became a woman. Years later he again saw two snakes mating, but this time he killed the male and became a man again. He thus knew what it was to be both man and woman.

The Sphinx is part woman, part dog, part serpent, and has a human voice. Oedipus wonders why, if Tiresias was around at the time, he could not have figured out the murderer of Laius. Good question. We might also ask why Tiresias had not come to the aid of Thebes and solved the riddle posed by the Sphinx. Tiresias is not an offspring of the Sphinx, but the myth of his mixed sexuality and his oracular powers would clearly make him a candidate to solve the riddle posed by this most powerful 'woman'.

But that might be too logical.

The myths that support and surround *Oedipus the King*, as well as the movement of the play itself, seem cannily orientated to the child's position in the world. Athenian mythology held that Gaia (the earth) and Ouranos (the sky) had intercourse, and that Gaia hid her offspring in the earth so that Kronos (time) would not eat them. Kronos ascended to power by cutting off his father's genitals. The drops of blood from the genitals became procreative acts, giving birth to the Furies and others. From the foam of the discarded genitals Aphrodite arose. Zeus, son of Kronos, later killed his father through an act of complicity with his mother.

It is little wonder that Sigmund Freud and Melanie Klein would insist that the epistemophilic drive begins with questions about sexuality. But, as they both emphasised, these are questions posed by the *child's* mind. The Sphinx is a nightmare of the child's imagination, an exemplar of the terrifying knowledge held by the adult, seemingly casting a plague on the child's life. As the child cannot know, his or her answers are informed by infantile projections that have a life of their own. The drive to know, then, carries the infantile element into the adult, who will later in life bring a certain innocence and imagination to the art of questioning. Thus infantile imaginative freedom and the cognitive powers of the adult mind combine to form the *interrogative element* that is part of the drive to know.

'Creon is no hurt to you, but you are to yourself,' says Tiresias to Oedipus, in what is probably the first psychoanalytic interpretation in the history of Western culture. Whatever be the slings and arrows of outrageous fortune, however much we suffer at the hands of others, Sophocles makes it clear that we are our own worst enemies.

Elsewhere I have argued that if the genius of man is to have a mind, it is also his curse.[42] Mental life raises countless questions, none more so than the dream. Freud showed how every night our unconscious weaves together a strange interpretation of the day's events, one that is often vivid enough to leave us wondering the next day: 'What was that about?'

As we have noted throughout this book, Freud took the challenge posed by the dream and formed it into a question that could be answered, at least in part, through the process of free association. But this turns out to be an endless process. In our youth we have the sense that our mental life can become understandable. As we age, however, this conviction is diminished by the infinite questions raised by dream after dream after dream.

endless process — endless analysis ?

By putting a patient and an analyst together in a room with the joint task of examining the dream of the analysand, Freud returned both participants to the place of the child. In confronting a dream as intelligent, educated, curious adults we find that the dream will always bear other interpretations, and the next night, and all the nights to follow, the sleeper will produce new dreams that will elaborate earlier ones, to produce – ultimately – the text of a lifetime. It is like living each day having read a new edition of Joyce's *Ulysses* the night before.

The dream is a mysterious object, a shadow of what Jean Laplanche terms the 'enigmatic signifier'. The discrepancy between the sophistication of the maternal unconscious and the undeveloped mind of the infant and child is a psychic reality that becomes a psychic structure. This rift between the wisdom of the other and our own ignorance creates a sense in us that we do not know what is taking place either within or without us.

This structure – a perpetual mental reality – leaves the subject bewildered. We cannot answer the questions that are posed by our own minds because the questioner is more complex than our consciousness can think. In my own work I have stressed that the dream is the most sophisticated form of thought we possess and exceeds our capacity to understand it, even though we shall always try. But it retains the function of the maternal enigmatic signifier, that other which will always keep us off balance, sustaining a rift between what we know and what is known by this other.

One of the tragedies of human life is that as we develop in time we realise that although we can 'grow up', our acquired wisdom does not displace that first reality, that the world around us is beyond our comprehension. Whilst in our childhood we questioned specific things, in old age we begin to occupy a different mental space. We come to appreciate the lineage of questioning itself. Very few single answers will last the test of time. The act of questioning seems, in the end, more fundamentally human than the production of answers. Looking back to the innocent questions of a child and then forward to the anxious

queries of the demented, we can find a link in the humanity of questioning.

Those questions posed in psychoanalysis arrive because
the interrogative position is a function of the unconscious.
The pressure of a question is driven by some unthought
knowledge which, for many possible reasons, is now ready
for unconscious thinking. Freud's model of repression directs
our attention to the return of unwanted ideas through a
derivative form, and there is no doubt that questions can
serve the purpose of facilitating such returns. But we cannot
restrict ourselves to the solitude of the repressed – there are
simply too many other, unrepressed, ideas within our
unconscious.

The unthought known is a form of knowledge that we
contain based on our earliest experiences of the object
world. Early meanings in human life, whether traumatic
or generative, cannot be thought. The meaning of what we
learn as infants, toddlers and small children is stored
within us in various forms – as images, as paradigms that
govern our assumptions, as moods that are part of the
orchestral effect of our character. Freud's theory of *après-
coup* states that the child is too young to bear the emotions
of powerful events and that the thinking of all early
experience is deferred. Only later in life – in a kind of
second coming – will stored affect be registered, often by
attaching itself to a minor life experience. From our adolescence onwards we are therefore visited continually by
arrivals from early lived experience. In an analysis these
arrivals take the form of trains of thought that we follow.
They are in fact driven by the force of knowledge, but
one that inevitably brings with it the question: what does
this mean?

The knowledge that drives questions, the dreams that
drive free associations, the day experiences that drive new
lines of thought: these and other mental phenomena that
lead to insights, realisations and mental development occur
unconsciously. The conscious self is now in the place of the
child who does not know, who cannot think the experiences
of being, while it is the unconscious self that carries the
wisdom of the self's history and engages in the deep work of

processing the details of lived experience through the symphony of unconscious thought.

These plays by Sophocles and Shakespeare follow the same logic. They seem to pose obvious questions – Why the plague? Who's there? – but these are rhetorical questions that signify the function of questioning itself: that is to say, what do I know that hasn't been thought yet?

The cases presented in Chapters 7–9 illustrate this view. Each of the analysands seems to begin the session with a question, then, as the hour proceeds, the interrogative form releases answers that seem, retrospectively, to have been initiated and driven by unconscious knowledge.

As conscious beings, then, psychoanalysis will always surprise us because it is one of the few spaces in which this oddity is forever encountered. In the early part of the twenty-first century many books have appeared that deal with aspects of consciousness; very few have been written on the unconscious. Yet it seems somewhat arrogant of consciousness to presume such a central position. How much do we know about our processes of thought? So little that we can find ourselves, it seems, reduced to a concrete action of show and tell. Like small children we point to models of the brain and indicate those parts where we can demonstrate certain mental activities taking place. This is akin to understanding the culture of a country by pointing out its geography.

Indeed, a hundred years or so after the publication of *The Interpretation of Dreams*, we know little more of the nature of unconscious thinking. I hope that the sessions we have read in this book – limited as they are – may allow us to see how Freud's early vision of the mind challenges us to think further about how and why people are *driven* to work unconsciously, to seek realisations, insights and, above all, psychological change. Each of the analysands presented here illustrates how the problems on our minds are the objects of deep unconscious work. Although we shall always resist certain recognitions, no resistance can outlast the dense power of the quest for knowledge. Most of our unconscious understanding will never become conscious;

transformation to consciousness should not be regarded as the measure of insight.

I remember listening to a recording of William Faulkner discussing his work. He was asked about one of his novels: what did he think was going on? He had no idea, Faulkner said: he just wrote them. There was not a hint of disingenuousness about his comment, although there was an unmistakable air of irritation. Faulkner – the writer who took stream of consciousness to its limits – was stating the obvious. From a conscious point of view he really did not know what to say about what he had created. Psychoanalysts would argue that the works derived from his unconscious creativity – and that really does mean unconscious. Writers, composers, painters and other creative people will all tend to state that they do not know where their ideas come from. In general only a minority are intellectually interested in discussing the process of creating their work, and when they do so, their attempts at conscious explanation are usually banal, pale companions to the works themselves.

Freud's concept of free association reveals a method that explores meaning through the intrinsically *interrogative drive* of the associative. As the analysand is speaking, he or she does not know why this idea, or the next one, or the next one, is occurring; but a willingness to accept this lack of conscious rationale remains an essential part of the drive to continue the associative process.

When Winnicott met with mothers and their babies – some thirty thousand of them during his career at St Mary's Hospital – he played his now famous 'spatula' gambit. He would place a spatula on the table in full view of the infant who, typically, would gaze at it briefly and then turn away. Then the infant would return to look at the object again with intense interest, often accompanied by drool. Winnicott termed this interval between the first and second look 'the period of hesitation'.

A book could be written about this simple but telling observation alone. One thing Winnicott noted was how a lived experience needed transformation through a second gaze, one that had internalised the sight of the presented object and had gathered a wish for it to reappear. In this

One must be willing to accept meaninglessness — at the center of one's life and work.

early example of *fort–da* the object is lost in order that it might be discovered through the illusion provided by infantile creativity.

Freud's method of free association understands this necessity brilliantly. He knew that the dreamer needs to turn away from the manifest content of the dream. Free associating to the dream occurs in a potential space, during a period of hesitation – one that might take hours or days – that enables the analysand to discover this dream's psychic significance. In the same way, free-associating analysands turn away from the large questions facing them in life and instead simply talk about what is on their minds. This turning away creates the same potential space that Winnicott discovered to be so essential to primary creativity. The analysand turns away not to avoid discovery of meaning but, on the contrary, to release his or her own unconscious perceptions to act upon the materials of consciousness, so that the resident meaning can be released from the apparent.

Winnicott argued that the period of hesitation was essential to the arrival of the infant's true self-experiencing. If he pushed the object towards the infant or otherwise encouraged the infant to look at it, this merely resulted in compliance – the logic of the false self. Freud's permission, that the analysand could cease to focus on so-called Freudian issues and just talk about life, illustrated the same genius.

The infant sees an object but does not yet know its experience. Implicit in the infant's turning away is a question – what is this? – a question that is arriving out of the spontaneity of the moment. Similarly, free-associating analysands find something, an idea that comes to mind, but they do not know what they think about what they have experienced. As they talk on and on, however, there is a gathering sense that the subtext of such meanderings consists of probing questions about what they know. It is the questioning form – both implicit and explicit – that drives our interest in our own knowledge.

One of our greatest philosophers, Socrates, understood the power of the question. Unlike Winnicott, however, Socrates did not allow those whom he interrogated a form of generative hesitation. Instead he destroyed the other's assumption of conscious truth, under the wave of question piling on question piling on question. His relentless exposure of consciousness to the infinite question may well have cost him his life.

The Socratic dialogue, however, aims to put into consciousness a relation between knowing and questioning that otherwise takes place unconsciously. If Plato's writings personify this relation through the figure of Socrates, who obviously had an unconscious grasp of the need for knowledge to have itself questioned, he failed to detect how the dialogue was an internal process, only rarely objectified through the act that would be termed philosophical investigation.

One of the reasons why all philosophical conclusions will inevitably be shattered by questions arising is that, as with all forms of thought, the answers we live by always raise questions that will inevitably carry us into new forms of knowledge. What Socrates took to be the method of philosophical investigation was instead a theatrical portrayal between two people (or more) of the way the mind works. It was a remarkable find, and he acted it out without, however, ever knowing what he had discovered.

In this book we have reviewed a theory of free association, and I have focused attention on what we can learn from it by presenting sessions from three patients. It is important to bear in mind that, in doing so, I have inevitably skewed our attention in a single direction, leaving out all the other complex phenomena at play in the clinical situation. I have not written here, for example, about character and character analysis. Nor have I discussed the transference and its relation to the countertransference, or the life instincts, drives and the drive derivatives. I have not focused on the idiomatic expressions of the analyst which inevitably constitute his or her action in the intersubjective field between the two participants, nor have I discussed the rich world of defence analysis.

I feel this concentration to be justified, however, by the refusal of so many analysts, over so many decades, to believe that free association exists. Perhaps the present book may help restore this cornerstone of psychoanalysis to its rightful place. If so, we may then turn towards further explorations of unconscious thinking. The interrogative function of our unconscious constantly works on that knowledge which we bear within ourselves as our unthought known, just as the force of this knowledge inspires intra-psychic curiosity.

for what?

An infinite question.

Appendix

The sessions that appear in Chapters 7–9 are presented here without commentary.

As noted in Chapter 6, it is recommended that the sessions are read in this form first – in a relaxed manner, perhaps a number of times, and without imposing any personal bias or preconceptions. Readers are advised not to try to 'figure out' what the analysands 'mean', but instead to see if a pattern of thought reveals itself over time.

After appraisal of the sessions in this form, the cases can then be read together with their commentaries in Chapters 7–9.

Arlene

Arlene comes through the door and greets the analyst. She says that she tried calling several times the previous day but the phone did not seem to work. She asks if there was something wrong with the phone, as it did not pick up. She says that perhaps she didn't 'persist' long enough, as eventually it turned out fine. She goes into the room and lies on the couch. There is a short silence.

Analyst: The incident with the phone seems a follow-on from our last session: how can one be heard?

Arlene: *(nods and then speaks slowly)* Yesterday . . . our choir went to the president of the Conservatory and talked to her. Because every girl in the group has a problem with the voice teacher. And she gave in at last, and we are allowed now to sing alone, without the voice teacher, every Sunday night. *(pauses)* As our choir met yesterday, they said that I should be the one who should do the talking. *(pauses)* It was very difficult for me because I do not like conflicts . . . or I try to avoid them. *(pauses)* Even if someone says something which is completely unacceptable or if someone is totally impolite . . . I don't answer back. *(pauses)* Yesterday was more than enough for me . . . and I don't know why, but even if someone understands that a person has a problem talking then people want exactly this person to do the talking. *There is silence for three or four minutes before Arlene continues.*
This was the same as with my parents . . . This is why I got into that subject again. The president of the Conservatory didn't want to hear what we actually had to say. *(pauses)* With some people you have to persist for a very, very, very long time on something, you have to repeat yourself all the time. You have to try to get their *real* attention. Or you hope that the problem will be solved by itself. Or if I say something once, then I don't say anything any more after that. *Another silence of three minutes follows.*

Analyst: Is that something you know in other ways too concerning yourself, that you 'do not say anything after that'?

Arlene: Yes . . . it is very often for me like that. Even when something comes to a conflict, I do not have my own opinion. I cannot come up with one. So if somebody says to me something then I take it for granted that it is so. And actually, in my profession this is risky because you do have to hold your position. You don't say to the other person, actually what you say seems very sensible and I agree with you.

Analyst: What if you do say what you think?

Arlene: Well, if I do not comply, then I make everything much worse. That is my thought. *(pauses)* I don't know where that comes from. My mother has been saying it to me all the time: anybody can come and you will follow him . . . But I somehow think that my mother talked me into it for so long that I came to believe it myself.

Analyst: That is an interesting insight. *Another silence of four minutes follows.*

Analyst: So this has been your way of avoiding conflict in your life?

Arlene: Yes, as long as I remember I have been like this.

Analyst: You are thinking . . . ?

Arlene: As a little child I would avoid conflicts of all kinds. I did not quarrel with other kids. I wasn't aggressive and I did not defend myself. *A short silence ensues before Arlene continues.* That is not strictly true. I would give an opinion, but if someone said something else I would not oppose it. I just don't know where that comes from. My sister can do it much better. I think I just did not develop in some ways after I was a child, but I don't know. My sister was outspoken.

Analyst: You have asked where the 'you' that speaks just once came from, and you follow it through with thoughts about your sister. After her arrival, I expect you felt gutted. You did not feel like talking.

Arlene: Um . . . *(pauses)* She is stronger than I am. She was able to work with my cousin. At the age of five or six I wasn't spoken to because my mother was never there and my father didn't bother with me anyway. There were always guests in the hotel, always needing my parents. And my mother never spoke with me. When we moved out of our first flat, we lived for a short while in a large hotel. My mother was gone the whole day long, even in the evenings . . . She went to the English Institute to improve her English so that she and my father could open their own hotel. And I remember that my sister was occupied with my cousin . . . and I couldn't communicate with her at that time because I didn't sign. She was nearly deaf and my sister could speak to her by signing. I couldn't speak the deaf language.

Analyst: You did not speak the deaf language.

Arlene: No, I don't know why.

Analyst: Well, you may have a theory. Following the line of your thought, your mother did not talk to you and so perhaps you thought that there was no point in speaking to someone who was deaf to your presence.

Arlene: I had not thought of it that way, but I see what you mean.

Analyst: I believe I have followed what you've said, but you might want to correct me.

Arlene: No. I see that these are in fact my thoughts, but just thinking out loud I wasn't thinking. I mean, I didn't know what it means.

Analyst: That happens a lot in this room.

Arlene: I am remembering my early school years. Neither of my parents asked . . . how is it in kindergarten, or do you have friends, or how is it with the English children . . . And I still remember the only incident where my mother did something with me alone . . . I was eight or nine years old and she read excerpts from a story about a girl who fell in love with a boy who spurned her, and later, when he was

in love with her, it was too late. I didn't understand
many things. She should have noticed from the way I
spoke Greek. And it is at any rate a very difficult
passage. She should have understood that I couldn't
understand it. And it was really the only thing that
my mother ever did with me.

There is silence for two minutes.

Analyst: The girl and the boy missed each other.

Arlene: Yes.

Analyst: Like . . . ?

Arlene: My mother and I. *(she cries)* I think the move
separated us. Then my sister was born. And then my
mother and father fell out with one another.

Analyst: Which made matters worse for you.

Arlene: I don't think my mother ever explained
anything to me. She indicated that she should not feel
obliged to explain things. For example, the story she
told me . . . She would say: 'At this age you should be
able to speak it, your Greek is enough. What is wrong
with you?'

*Another silence of four minutes follows before Arlene
continues.*

I can remember when my father went to this other
town to do catering. Each Sunday when he returned
home to Leeds I said I didn't want to go to school the
next day, so I could spend a day with him because he
was in Leeds on Mondays. I pretended to have these
headaches. I did the same thing with my mother. I
would tell her I wasn't feeling well so that when she
was around I could stay with her. Then he stayed in
this other town and rarely came home.

Analyst: It was very painful to have been left by each of
them. I think you must have felt quite lost.

Arlene: Yes.

Analyst: So you complied. You obviously felt you could
not say that you wanted to go to the other town to
stay with your father?

Arlene: I think I lacked the courage. My mother always
said he was so bad, so that she would say: 'What? You
want to stay with your horrid father?'

Analyst: And you must have been afraid she would say that she would have nothing further to do with you.
Another silence of three minutes follows.

Arlene: My sister told me recently, that I was left alone very often as a child. She remembered it very well . . .

— Even when my mother was present, she was so involved in her own things that she didn't talk, she didn't say anything.
There is a silence of two minutes before Arlene continues.

— My mother was so intimidating.

Analyst: Do you suppose this answers something of the riddle you have been thinking of in this session? Of

— wondering why you say something just once and not again, because you do not want conflict, and hope problems will just solve themselves?

Arlene: I think that is right. In fact, at the time, when mother would yell at me, I would feel or say – or both

→ – 'Well, that's it: you said it, but nothing will happen.' I was afraid of her. I did not want to make conflict. But . . . *(it happened anyway)*
Arlene pauses and then stirs on the couch.
Well, after a while I did see my father. My mother forbade it, but I found a way and so did he and so we did manage.

Analyst: Ah. So that's persistence! You persisted in telephoning, you persisted in pursuing your father, so you have a quiet belief that persistence is the thing, which must have been there when you insisted to the president of the Conservatory that the choir did not need a voice teacher.

Arlene: Yes. I suppose that is right.

Analyst: Um.

Arlene stands up, greets the analyst with a smile and a handshake, and leaves.

(about herself)

SbS was reading this. 8/19

Caroline – Session 1

Caroline: I had a dream last night. I had invited several
guests. But I hadn't prepared or bought anything, so
there was nothing to drink or eat in the fridge. I went
to my neighbour, Marge. She usually has a good
collection of wine. I asked her whether she could help
me. But she said she seemed not to have the wine
after all and so she could not be of help.

I don't like to shop or prepare things for guests.
At home usually I have nothing in the fridge.
Yesterday Edward came home at ten o'clock in the
evening and I couldn't offer him anything to eat. I
was ashamed. But I hadn't thought that he might be
hungry.   *others might be in wait*

He, unlike me, always has something in the
fridge. He is a great cook and sometimes prepares
wonderful meals for me.   *mechanical*

He is also a very good guide. When we hike in the
Fens he is always well orientated. He looks at the
map and then knows where we have to take our
route. It's not worth it for me to try to do something
like that by myself, so I leave it up to him and like to
be guided by him.

Analyst: In your dream Marge hasn't said anything   *no guide*
helpful for you . . .

Caroline: Marge is from Scotland. She is the friend of a
colleague from university. Both are painters. They
spend a lot of time abroad. The two always complain
about not having enough money. They feel   *others in want*
disadvantaged in relation to people who earn more
money than they do and blame them. They have an
ideal utopia . . .

Marge is on one side very lively and enjoys life,   *self*
but on the other very frustrated, because she claims *portrait*
she is not getting enough recognition, which she
would have deserved.

Oh yes . . . recognition . . . I had a clash with the
secretary of the psychopharmacology institute, where
Edward works as an assistant. I wanted to go to a

small congress they organise. I had missed the date
for subscription. The secretary told me that there
were already 120 participants instead of 90, which
were planned. It would be impossible to get admission
for me. I said that I'm Edward's partner – but she
said this wouldn't matter, and that I should stop
being so pushy.

When Edward came home, he told me that she
went to him and warned him. She said that I was
trying to take advantage of Edward's position and
that this was an exploitation of our relationship. She
told him to stop me. I went completely mad when I
heard this. Who does this woman think I am? I was
incensed . . . If someone like her puts a limit in front
of me it enrages me. That she says I complained is
impossible – and that she calls Edward.

In the dream I already switched the points
wrongly – I invited without having prepared
anything.

Analyst: You don't want to need to do something like
that.

Caroline: And I *didn't want* to pay for the congress – it
was even the most expensive price because I was too
late. I wanted to ask the university where I work
whether they would pay for me. Honestly, *they* should
invite *me* to the congress without letting me pay!
They should invite me as a *guest of honour*!

In the dream, when it badly threaded it doesn't
work any more. I can't help myself, not even with
Marge.

Analyst: The question is, why is it badly threaded? Why
did you invite your guests without having prepared
anything? Perhaps preparing something would mean
not being a guest of honour, just a normal person.

Caroline: I hoped, *somehow*, that there would be a good
solution, without me *doing anything*. I was *sure* that
the Dean of Studies would be *very pleased* when he
saw me. The secretary should have made it possible
that I could participate, even if I didn't subscribe on
time. I'm really very upset about having to pay £90. I

but not to act!

am absolutely sure that I want to participate. It's only because of this *damn* secretary that I cannot be admitted.

By the way, at the Yoga Centre I didn't pay either . . .

Analyst: You think your special admission there works ?
through me . . .

Caroline: Well, I think I don't have to pay like everybody else there. Perhaps it's a test: whether they would kick me out or not. I am pleased that Edward now must do something, to make it possible — that I can take part at the congress.

not doing to force the other to prove

Caroline – Session 2

Caroline: That was a strange session last time.
There is silence for two minutes.
— Today I went first to your old address, to Kensington
High Street. I was so much involved in talking to you
in my mind that I went to the old office. I'm so tired of
all the dates, which determine my life. And I'm fed up
with my work at the research centre.

Well in the last session we talked about my
admission to the congress and the parallel situation
at the Yoga Centre. Afterwards I was astonished
about the urge to have a special status. It reminds me
of all the things which I couldn't bear about my friend
Rina, who always wanted to be someone special. I
thought, it is because of this need of being someone
special that I'm still in analysis and have difficulties
thinking of this ending.

Analyst: So ending analysis for you means losing this
special status?

Caroline: Playing the piano was my special relation to
my aunt. Giving up piano was like betraying my aunt.
When I stop analysis here, my connection to you will
break, which is a guarantee for something else. My
relation to you contains something of my self.

Analyst: Because I listen to you . . .

Caroline: Yes – but it is the guarantee for having access
to something very important, which I can't have
otherwise without you.
*A silence of two minutes follows before Caroline
continues.*
I didn't choose you because of your status at the
Psychoanalytical Society. I even didn't know about it
when I chose you. I chose your name because I liked
it. I went to another analyst who had her practice
nearer to my flat. But I liked your address too:
Kensington High Street. When I had seen you both,
I knew that you and I would fit.

In some way I find access to myself in your
presence. And I don't find it when I'm alone.

I found the same access to myself in the presence of my aunt. She contained something precious of me, as you do too.

Analyst: You mean, you were someone special for her, as you think to be for me. *carefully he does not say he is*

Caroline: Creativity and all sorts of self-expression were the most important things in life for my aunt. She was happy about every personal expression of mine, be it piano, telling stories or whatever. And in some way I experience the same here with you.

A silence of one minute follows before Caroline continues.

I had also the same name as my aunt had.

She thought a lot about deep themes, about life and great literature. I felt life as uncanny but also thrilling, and I liked to discuss deep questions with my aunt.

I experienced her as very young and mobile – she discussed with me the questions which one has in adolescence. I had chosen my aunt as my highest ideal. *why*

At her side I disappeared. I didn't see myself any more, because she was in the centre of my attention. There is always this conviction in me that I wouldn't be able to develop something inside of me, that I wouldn't be able to live something for which I have the potential. *not prepare*

Analyst: Your aunt and I have to help you with this.

Caroline: Yes, but analysis is precisely this – don't you think so? *(asking for leader)* *like a constellation*

Analyst: Analysis is also what you will take with you when you leave me. *saying, you will lead*

A silence of five minutes follows before the analyst continues.

You're silent.

Caroline: Me alone and my unconscious – this is not enough. It needs two. Otherwise my unconscious becomes dominant. My fate, that I don't bring out something which is sticking inside me . . . above all when I'm alone, I won't get it out . . . *?*

Yesterday I took a mirror of my aunt's. It belonged to my sister. I robbed this mirror from my sister's flat and took it to my place. I felt so guilty about robbing again. And about being so materialistic.

Analyst: Robbing must have something to do with not being able to get out what is inside you. Perhaps you can let it out here because you are sure that I won't be critical of you.

Robbing = special status

Robbing = not preparing

Annie – Session 1 (Monday)

Annie: The weather was so beautiful over the weekend. I spent a lot of time in the garden. I emailed Marcus about how I went and bought a marigold plant and how I felt like I was setting it free. I freed it from the little pot it was in.
For the next minute or two she describes in fine detail everything she did to prepare it for planting.
It was fun and muddy.

Analyst: And a nice metaphor . . .

Annie: Mmm. I bought it because it had a bloom. I've been wanting to tell you how good you look lately. Like life must be agreeing with you in some way. It seems you've changed a fair amount since we started this analysis. Last autumn you seemed to get bogged down a bit, but whatever that was, it's gone. Your colour is good.

Analyst: You seem more free to say that now.

Annie: Yes, though I'm not saying directly that I'm interested in you and the 'I wish . . .' sorts of things. It's more 'I appreciate.' I got asked for my driving licence yesterday and told the policeman, 'Oh, you're handing out random acts of kindness, are you?' Once that happened when I was travelling and I wouldn't give my ID to the guy. I was being playful and said to him, 'You just want to know something about me.'

Well, I had a real reaction to Marcus's attention to me, as you saw on Friday. It was old stuff, and threw me back, which I didn't like. I was talking about it with Carlos, who had an intense reaction to my reaction, to my feeling lesser than Marcus in some way, Marcus being such an accomplished person. He seems to have his head on straight. He's a success. Then Carlos asked me if I think of him as successful. I told him, 'You seem to think you're not – you seem not happy with what you have.' So he took that overnight as 'I think of him as a non-success.' He emailed the next morning, saying he couldn't live with having a friend who thought of him this way. He lashed out at me for who I put on pedestals. Some of it hit home.

In some ways he was right, that putting Marcus on a pedestal will make it hard for me to relate to him. I cried for a while thinking about it. I emailed back. He called me later, still smarting that I said he was stupid. I said to him: 'You're not fighting against me but somebody else – you're pinning things on me I don't feel. What's this about? Your mother?' He just let loose and said, 'Oh, God, I just remembered something I haven't thought about in years.' Long story short, he remembered his mum had called him 'stupid' frequently, and now he was connecting this to his issue of thinking he's not bright. Apparently, his mother couldn't recognise any intelligence in him. I told him: '*Please* take this to your analyst!' He said he would if he could remember to.

He came over later and helped me with my studio. It needed to be braced. We worked on it together and he was trying to figure out the angles of the wood he was cutting. He used a protractor. I had an idea and said, 'Would this work?', but it didn't. Then I had another idea that did work. I'm watching him at this point and not wanting to correct him; I felt like I was figuring it out but should let him figure it out for himself, which he did. Spatially, he does have limits on how he thinks and I think very well spatially. I didn't want to let him know. Then at dinner he said, 'You're really good at solving spatial problems.' I said, 'Well, I'm a film-maker.' Anyway, I do have a tendency to put people up on pedestals, so with that thought I emailed Marcus back as an ordinary person, in grief from a terrible loss. Now, he wants to get together.

It was painful with Carlos. Both our issues hit in the same spot so it took a while to figure out.

I figured it out while I was shopping for marigolds. I still want to find somebody like you.

I really don't think I'm putting you on a pedestal, but I don't know how you are in life outside here. Yet

depressive position vignette

gratitude

I do know how you are in here. I don't think I would
have figured out what I did without what we've gone
through in here guided by you. A relationship outside
here would have more equality maybe . . . It seems to
have gone in both directions here. The feeling is I'd
like to try it in the other way.

herself
be the
stronger

figure = give person to

Analyst: It *is* a good feeling to figure something out.

Annie: It kind of illuminates the difficulties I had with
James. That didn't happen enough. If this had been
James and I was bumping up, he'd have said: 'This is
what I have to have – you *must not* think of me as
unsuccessful.' Carlos listened, heard something and
figured it out. And I figured something out too. Maybe
I'm willing to accept more responsibility. That was
hard to do with James because he wouldn't accept
any. So I had to take a defensive posture.

I had a dream on Saturday night. At work, in real
life, Ines has had a rough pregnancy and ended up
having a caesarean. In my dream, I was with her. Oh,
the first thing she said was: 'I have a fever – I don't
feel well.' I knew she was going into labour. I asked
the doctor if that was normal. He said 'yes'. So the
delivery started. I could feel her intense strong pain,
then it was normal, then again I could feel the
intensity. Instead of a caesarean, she actually gave
birth.

birth

It seems straightforward. There's the marigold,
the birth. The pain about Marcus and Carlos was like
a birthing pain. Essential. *(pauses)* I was disturbed
by something you said at the end on Friday. It felt
like I sometimes feel when teaching, as if I'm having
a hard time getting into the depths and doing the
figuring, and it was like you were saying I was
struggling with something that had already been
figured out and so I was sliding backwards. You
weren't helping me. You were frustrated with me,
like, 'Hasn't she got that yet?'

one
pain

related
pain

I did something this morning. I read James's
email. Right away I saw a message from the woman I
think he picked up with right away after I moved out.

She said in this poetic way, 'Let's each make love with whomever and watch and grade the lover.' That's a really interesting concept! What is James thinking and feeling? To do that, he would have to let go of some of that rigidity he has. It piques my interest what he would do with such an offer. So I want to know, has anyone ever offered that to you?

Analyst: It makes me wonder if you're thinking about the voyeuristic part of being a therapist.

(deflecting)

Annie: You're right. I hadn't thought of that. You hear back whole descriptions of people's experience. That's interesting. But it's for a different purpose – at least we hope so. That immediately brings up how people have been commenting on how voyeuristic my new work is. I'm doing houses in neighbourhoods, especially the windows. Usually I get a reflection, but it feels a little like an encroachment sometimes. I've been filming a lot this week.

Analyst: We talked a good deal on Friday about how you expect I will feel threatened by your thoughts of me having a family, as if there's a danger or 'watch out' in the air.

I simply analyze, no danger + her early wish to see

M has the dangerous family

Annie: It's different between you and Marcus. With him it was more of an overwhelm. I plugged into all the difficulties there would be with him having a family, including ones that aren't even on the table, like the fact that his teenage boys know more scholastically than I do. Now that I'm getting clearer about it, there's Marcus's mind in front of me and I get to have access to it. With your family it felt more like I might destroy something, not meaning to. But at the same time maybe I want to a little bit. You have a wife, so to interject myself there would be to destroy something.

Analyst: And Marcus doesn't have a wife any more.

Annie: I'm afraid I'd get in there and mess it all up. Mess up what he's built with his children and the lives they have. Like I'm a cancer.

Annie – Session 2 (Tuesday)   *responsibility*

Annie: I was thinking about what we talked about at
the end yesterday. It seems right. I was taken back
to what my psychologist said to me at nineteen
years old – that I felt I was responsible for my
parents' divorce. I heard that, but I didn't yet see
how it transformed into how I acted with Marcus.
Everything is there.

Carlos said to me, 'When I talk about politics, you
tune out.' I said, 'Yes, I do space out.' He asked me
why and I thought about my dad.

There was the blowout at the dinner table every
night between him and my stepmother and her
friend. Night after night the argument got too heated.
Politics, to me, represents anger. The other thing is,
my stepmother. I don't know much about Buddhism,
but her way of practising it was to lord it over us.
Marcus is a Buddhist. He's casual in his practice. And
he has three sons. And he is a maths prodigy.

In my first marriage, my husband spent a lot of
time with his mother after his father died during our
honeymoon.

I wanted to pull away and be a satellite. I didn't
know how to be anything else. That's why I feel I
might mess it up. I talked to Marcus last night. We're
set to have lunch a week from tomorrow. That gives
me way too much time to think about things. I'm
getting the cyst off tomorrow.   *something coming off – OK*

I felt like a satellite at the family reunion last
summer. People didn't seem to want to get into it. I
was talking with my stepmum and her maid came
into the room to check on her to see if she was okay! It
feels like if I *were* accepted, I wouldn't know what to
do with it, wouldn't know how to act. Marcus seems to
desperately need to touch something. Not physically.
He has that hole where his wife used to be. There was
a lot of conversation every day and now no one's
there. He asked if he could come down and see my
marigold.

Tess came over yesterday. She did four hours of film editing. It was helpful. She seems alive now, versus when I taught her. She told me about the surgery she had: she had excess skin cut off. Then the drainage tubes got infected. Then the antibiotics led to grand mal seizures. Now she looks bright and alive. She's normal weight but has these huge scars. *A pause of a few minutes follows before Annie continues.*

When Carlos and I went through that at the weekend I was getting that feeling about me – as toxic.

Analyst: What is it like?

Annie: Like rather than being the kind of person who supports, I try to hold them back. Unwittingly, I figure out their issues and play on them. This is an overt example: Maggie is adopting a child. She went in, was tested, and was told she has a 'horned uterus'. Depending on how it's horned it can be okay or dangerous for having a child. After that, I heard she was trying to adopt, but I haven't talked to her about it. Then I had another conversation with someone in James's apartment building, called Susan, who was telling me all about the fibroids in her uterus. Loudly. She then left down the hallway to find her boyfriend and it turns out he'd been sitting right around the corner listening to her talk about her uterus looking like a gourd. I later told Maggie about this conversation with Susan and as soon as the words came out, I realised how insensitive it was, even though I was using the conversation to illustrate how obnoxiously loud Susan was. Subconsciously, I do this to people – that's why I'm toxic.

Analyst: You talk about your feelings as though they are so intertwined with other people's lives that it's as though you have some responsibility . . .

Annie: I see that with the one big fight my parents had when I was eleven, that made me feel responsible for the divorce. My father stayed in the area for a year or so and then moved pretty far away, to Wales. I must have felt there was nothing I could do to keep him here. I wasn't enough. Therefore I had to have done something wrong. Had I done it right, he would've stayed. I think he may still feel some guilt about it. I don't think we talked on the phone much after he left, but I don't really have memory of it. I may have been hard to talk to on the phone – not much to say. My self as a child was watching and quiet.

Analyst: You portray it as manipulative, but from the sound of it, with Carlos over the weekend, you didn't have to do much to tap into that in him.

Annie: That's right, there was definitely projection going on with that. When he told his analyst about it, apparently they talked about how his last relationship that failed had the same push–pull as he had with his mother. He said, 'leave me alone', but if she did he wasn't okay with that either. It was the first time I saw a glimmer of him saying *he'd* done something to *her*. So it was interesting. I suppose the thought to consider is that I'm not God, to be as toxic as I think I am.

Did you ever see that movie, *Badlands*? Sissy Spacek and Martin Sheen. They're young and he kills her father to get her, so they end up on the road as waifs, being looked for and hiding. And they get into situations where he keeps killing. She is horrified by it but sticks with him. I've thought about this a lot, that the evil in the world is often a combination of two. Like Myra Hindley and her lover. Something was created by the two of them that brought out this . . . I think when I'm . . . When I look at James, did we freeze each other? Is who I am part of what threw him into the rigidity? We went in a toxic direction rather than moving in another direction. I don't know. A lot of things reinforced it. The divorce, my father leaving, my mother's treatment of me. I was too sexual with other kids at school. But I wasn't toxic with my half-brothers ever, though my stepmother thought I was.

Analyst: We've talked about this for a long time up till now without calling it this. *What does this reply do?*

Annie: Last year, intensely so. I thought you were starting a new family and there were changes in the schedule [of sessions]. My feelings were strong about wanting you, and while you were starting a family I wasn't and couldn't. It's backwards. I wanted you to drop that and be with me – yet that would have been the toxic thing. It's funny, I feel really sleepy.

Analyst: What do you make of it?

Annie: It's a shutdown. Everything gets so heavy. Visiting my dad's family, I'd sleep a lot. I wanted the day to go by so I wouldn't have to be in it. Overload. Something to do with being a teenager too. I disappeared. Maybe that's what the sleep is. I could disappear. Because if I'm not there people won't have to go away. If I don't do anything then things won't change. In my nightmares I was worried about my mum being taken away and being left with nothing. Maybe this has to do with the mirror also. The mirror was moving when I wasn't, which meant that I couldn't control something. But I was also inert. Since I couldn't control it, I had to be inert or I would lose my mother too. That goes with the dream where I'm a larva.

Analyst: If you weren't there at least things wouldn't get worse.

Annie: Right. I was scared to do or say *anything*. I think that goes with why I was trying to hide my broken arm: 'I'm not injured, go away, don't pay attention!' It made me noticeable.

The session ends, ten minutes late.

Annie – Session 3 (Wednesday)

Annie: I feel much better today. I went to film after yesterday's session but I couldn't. I felt the light wasn't right. It was too hot and nothing was presenting itself. And I was still tired. So I went home and had a nap. Then I went to class. I enjoyed it. Only four of the seven students were there. The missing ones were all juniors. It was actually very nice. I was very concrete with them. I told them: 'I'm giving you a specific assignment – if you do it, you get an A; if you don't, you get an F. The assignment is to go to the art library and find a painting, any painting, that is new to you, bring it in and say what struck you.' (*pauses*) I don't know if you went over time yesterday on purpose because things were intense or if you made a mistake, but I was glad it happened. In those few minutes, a lot went on. I kind of appreciated it, mistake or not. My first concern was whether someone was out there waiting. If I'd had to wait ten minutes I'd have been upset. That leads to two other thoughts: the students last night wanted to stay past 10 p.m. editing their films. It was nice they wanted to stick around. Also, I talked to Marcus this morning. He told me how his middle child was helping the youngest with his Latin lessons. They were really involved in it. Then the oldest came into the room and they ignored him. So he went back out and did this comical thing with Marcus where he went on and on saying: 'I'm invisible! What if I went to school and no one could see me!' He's so social he couldn't bear it, but his little brother could. Funny he brought that up after our session, where I'd talked about being invisible.

To make it too simple: being with James let me stay in a comfortable–uncomfortable position of being invisible. It's interesting that when Mum died that position was no longer possible. Something in my connection with her made me need to be invisible.

Apparently, Tess has told all the teachers that she loves me, so now they're teasing me a little, saying, 'What do you do that we don't do?'

Analyst: And did you tell them?

Annie: *(smiling)* I'm supposed to know this? If anything, she needs not to be told what to do, but to be asked for information. For example, instead of 'Why are you doing this?' it needs to be 'How can you do this; the emotion is not in the film – how can you get it in there?' Her first ideas always seem as if they're not going to work. Kind of silly.

She loves herons. She drives to the Fens and films them. Her teachers say, 'Why are you doing this? Maybe you shouldn't do birds', etc. I said, 'What do you like about herons?' She thought about it and figured it out: 'I've had a heron collection since I was four years old. The first time I saw one was with my grandfather. I was transfixed by the herons. He kept feeding me little sandwiches while I looked. It brings me back to my whole grandfather experience. That's what I'm trying to save and keep.' I said to her, 'Okay, how are you going to do this?' and she came up with: 'I'll make the photos and films of my collected herons into a documentary, and will give them a description, then pair my film with an official film of herons.' I told her, 'You know, it will probably work. You're juxtaposing kitsch and beauty, the memory and the actual.' So she has a way of taking a silly idea and making it into something substantial. The teachers are trying to make her process be like what they want it to be. I told her differently, that her process is what it is. That's why she went and told everyone she was in love with me.

Analyst: You told her it's okay to go with her muse.

Annie: Yes, and everyone else is confused. I suspect that patients in analysis all go through their own patterns and it's a puzzle sometimes to try to figure it out. There *is* a framework to think about it in, but then you have the *patient*, and it becomes a whole different thing. I was going to ask you . . . It's a funny

question. I was thinking about the process I've gone
through here, from the beginning. The whole . . .
metamorphosis, I suppose. I was going to ask you
if there was a name for it.

Analyst: How do you think of 'metamorphosis'?

Annie: A change from one thing into another – from
larva to fully functioning insect! *(smiles)* The dreams
I had of my being a larva . . . I don't know if there's a
psychological concept for it, if you had to give it a
name. I'm interested in what *word* you would use.

Analyst: Honestly, my field tends to be dry in this area;
tends to think about these things in a too-linear way.

Annie: I've heard psychoanalysis can be 'finished', but
there's also a continuing investigation. There's never
a point where you get to the end because it's so
complex. It's funny, there's the book I told you about
once, *On Sleep*. It's about dreaming. My habit with
books is that I often start two or three, put them
aside, then finish them later. I couldn't believe what
it was saying. The writer is a rock climber, a dream
and visual researcher, Andrews maybe? It's
interesting that he would think about it as a whole
body–person engagement. Film-making is a little
that way. He talks about vision. If you just take the
physics of it, rods and cones are just a bunch of blobs.
It takes a brain putting it together to see what you
see. You learn from experience how to see. He's a
lucid dreamer. He was amazed a dream could
construct such rich visual experience. His interest
was how much does the brain contribute to sight.
Mice raised with no horizontal lines couldn't see them
as adults!

   Experience is so crucial to how you see. When I
took my first hit of acid I wondered, 'Is my light blue
someone else's light orange?' Experience may be
different between people, so you actually can make
films that are *yours* – personal.

Analyst: Hm.

Annie: His book seems like the pathway into that. The
art school I teach at stresses the assignment, not

what the student wishes to shoot. The book got really
exciting to read. If I could see through someone else's
eyes, how would it look? Suddenly I think you're
disagreeing.

Analyst: What is your thought?

Annie: You hesitated for a second when you said 'hm', as
if you were turning it over and questioning it rather
than accepting it, which is a reasonable thing to do I
suppose.

Analyst: I'm disappointed it came across that way and I
think we should give some thought to this. It gets me
wondering if you were maybe expecting
disagreement.

Annie: James would have to form his opinion and
espouse it right there. Or say the same thing I just
said in a different way. Or say no, then repeat what I
said. It became his. Never 'that's interesting, what
else did they say?' *Never, ever.*

Analyst: Almost as though you hadn't said anything
at all.

Annie: The word in the community is that he
appropriates everyone else's ideas without
acknowledging it was ever theirs first . . . I'm invisible
again! Being invisible with him became too much
for me.

The session ends.

Notes/References

1 In *Being a Character* (New York: Hill and Wang, 1992) I emphasised how real objects are evocative and how we use them not only because of their 'integrity' (as structures) but because they contain personal meaning (from the history of our projections), as well as social and cultural significance. When we use such objects we do not only play in the object world: we think certain thoughts through their continuing evocative effect.

2 Bollas, Christopher, 1992. *Being a Character*. New York: Hill and Wang, pp. 21–2.

3 Freud, Sigmund, 1900. *The Interpretation of Dreams, Standard Edition of the Complete Psychological Works of Sigmund Freud* V. London: Hogarth Press.

4 Freud, *The Interpretation of Dreams*, p. 84.

5 Freud, Sigmund, 1915. 'The unconscious', *Standard Edition of the Complete Psychological Works of Sigmund Freud* XIV. London: Hogarth Press.

6 Freud, Sigmund, 1923. *The Ego and the Id, Standard Edition of the Complete Psychological Works of Sigmund Freud* XIX. London: Hogarth Press.

7 Freud, *The Interpretation of Dreams*, p. 706.

8 Freud, *The Interpretation of Dreams*, p. 383.

9 Freud, 'The unconscious', p. 35.

10 Freud, *The Interpretation of Dreams*, p. 422.

11 Freud, *The Interpretation of Dreams*, p. 669.

12 Freud, *The Interpretation of Dreams*, p. 672.

13 Freud, *The Interpretation of Dreams*, p. 751.

14 Freud, *The Interpretation of Dreams*, p. 773.

15 Freud, *The Interpretation of Dreams*, p. 424.

16 Freud, *The Interpretation of Dreams*, p. 424.

17 Freud, *The Interpretation of Dreams*, p. 425.

18 Freud, *The Interpretation of Dreams*, p. 425.

19 Freud, *The Interpretation of Dreams*, p. 427 (my italics).

20 Freud, *The Interpretation of Dreams*, p. 780.

21 Breuer, Josef, and Freud, Sigmund, 1893–55. 'Studies on Hysteria' *Standard Edition of the Complete Psychological Works of Sigmund Freud* II. London: Hogarth Press, p. 290.

22 Freud, *The Interpretation of Dreams*, p. 282.

23 Freud, Sigmund, 1913. 'On Beginning the Treatment' *Standard Edition of the Complete Psychological Works of Sigmund Freud* XII. London: Hogarth Press, p. 134.

24 Freud, Sigmund, 1912. 'Recommendations to Physicians Practising Psycho-Analysis' *Standard Edition of the Complete Psychological Works of Sigmund Freud* XII. London: Hogarth Press, p. 112.

25 Freud, 'Recommendations to Physicians Practising Psycho-Analysis', pp. 115–16.

26 See *The Shadow of the Object* (London: Free Association Books, 1987), pp. 239–40; *Forces of Destiny* (London: Free Association Books, 1987), p. 202; *Being a Character* (New York: Hill and Wang, 1992), pp. 73–84; *Cracking Up* (New York: Hill and Wang, 1995), p. 31; *The Mystery of Things* (London: Routledge, 1999), pp. 181–95; *Hysteria* (London: Routledge, 2000), p. 72; *The Freudian Moment* (London: Karnac Books, 2007), pp. 27–30; *The Evocative Object World* (London: Routledge, 2008), pp. 47–77.

27 Vendler, Helen, 2006. *Poets Thinking: Pope, Whitman, Dickinson, Yeats*. Cambridge, MA: Harvard University Press, p. 5.

28 Vendler, *Poets Thinking*, p. 7.

29 Freud, Sigmund, 1923. 'Two encyclopaedia articles', *Standard Edition of the Complete Psychological Works of Sigmund Freud* XVIII. London: Hogarth Press.

30 See *The Mystery of Things* (London: Routledge, 1999), pp. 59–74; *The Freudian Moment* (London: Karnac Books, 2007), pp. 1–32; and *The Evocative Object World* (London: Routledge, 2008), pp. 7–13.

31 Freud, 'Two encyclopaedia articles', p. 238.

32 Freud, 'Two encyclopaedia articles', p. 239.

33 Freud, *The Interpretation of Dreams*, p. 680.

34 See Bollas, Christopher, 2007. *The Freudian Moment* (London: Karnac Books). Lacan also used the musical score as a metaphor of how one could read unconscious discourse: 'all discourse is aligned along the several staves of a musical score' (Lacan, Jacques, revised translation by Bruce Fink, 2002. *Écrits*, New York: W.W. Norton, pp. 146/504). I imagine the score as a means of representing categorically different forms of unconscious

articulation, including the actions of transference, or the movement of emotion, and so forth.

35 In Bion's theory, where K stands for knowledge, –K stands for a mental state organised to rid the self of its capacity to know.

36 Levitin, Daniel J., 2006. *This is Your Brain on Music: The Science of a Human Obsession*. New York: Dutton, pp. 103–4.

37 All quotations from *Oedipus the King* are from the David Grene (1942) translation.

38 Zimmerman, John Edward, 1983. *Dictionary of Classical Mythology*. New York: Bantam Books, p. 247.

39 All quotes from *Hamlet* are from the 1982 Arden Edition, edited by Harold Jenkins.

40 Zimmerman, *Dictionary of Classical Mythology*, p. 246.

41 See Bollas, Christopher, 1987. *The Shadow of the Object*. London: Free Association Books, pp. 157–69.

42 See Bollas, Christopher, 1999. 'Mind against self', in *The Mystery of Things*. London: Routledge.

Index

'deafness', maternal 39, 46, 51
death, sexuality and 91
defences 52, 114–15; sleepiness 95,
    101, 102; thinking through
    resistances and 83
defiance: of silence 47; towards the
    mother 43, 45, 47
depression 50, 133, 134
derivatives xi, 14, 16, 39, 148
'descriptive unconscious' 17
desire, revealed by serial logic 6
destructiveness: feelings of being
    cancerous/toxic 85, 86–7, 92, 93,
    94–5, 100–1; of the primal scene
    94; see also messing up
differentiation: acting out a form of
    separation 61; defying the
    mother 43, 45, 47; fear of 43;
    idealisation and 66–7, 70–1
dissociation 101, 109
doubt 22
dramatic order of representation
    59, 60, 74; see also enactment
dream work: free association
    reporting 9–11, 56, 59, 73, 82;
    Freud's theory 17; projective
    thinking 57, 69–70; and the
    return to the place of the child
    147; unconscious dream-working
    of the analyst 99
dreams: censoring of 1, 2;
    condensation 1, 2, 10; dream-
    thoughts 1, 3–4, 5, 22; dream
    work see dream work; formation
    mechanism ix, 1, 3, 16, 127–8,
    146; and the maternal enigmatic
    signifier 147; nightmares 96–7;
    questions raised by 56, 128,
    146; temporal logic/sequence
    5–6, 17
dynamic unconscious 2–3

echoing 123
ego 129; splitting 57;
    transformational objects and the
    grammar of the ego xiv
emotion: affective power of
    associations 79–80; dispossession
    of emotional depth by manic
    thought 82–3, 109, 111;
    emotional development 108–9;

feeling special 62, 64, 70;
    linking of emotions to ideas 17,
    59; splitting off affects and
    instincts 96; and the theory of
    après-coup 148; understood
    through revelation of its logic
    26
empathy 46; empathic assistance
    108; passive empathic responses
    124
enactment: enacting the self 59, 74;
    as form of communication 116;
    maternal 37, 43; through a
    parallel analysis 90; see also
    dramatic order of representation
enigmatic signifiers 147
epistemophilic drive 141, 144–5,
    146; of the infinite question 142,
    153
evenly suspended attention/
    attentiveness 20, 31–2, 54, 126,
    135
evocative objects x, 179n1
explicit questions 22, 54
extractive introjection 145

facial expression 25
faecal imagery 78, 86–7, 101,
    104–5, 107, 110
fathers/the paternal: identification
    with the father 134–5; loss of 41,
    53; the paternal order of the
    social world 61; repression and
    15; sex and the killing of the
    father 91; superego as the
    forbidding father 15
Faulkner, William 150
feelings: of being cancerous/toxic
    85, 86–7, 92, 93, 94–5, 100–1 see
    also emotion; evacuation of 98;
    intertwined with others' lives 93,
    104; of specialness 62, 64, 70; see
    also emotion
fetishism, of sexuality and
    aggression 2–3, 4
figuring out 80–1, 83, 86, 98, 103,
    113
flippancy 114
flirting 114
forgotten material 135
fort–da 150–1

splitting 57; surgical removal of 76, 92, 99, 113; that raise doubt 22; theft of 67–8, 70–1; transformational xiv
Oedipal child 44
Oedipal transcendence 109
Oedipus complex 141
Oedipus the King (Sophocles) 139–42, 144, 145, 146
omnipotent thought/demands 44, 47
the other: articulation of the Other 98; the facilitating other 109; fear of merging with the other 72; guidance by 56–7, 66–7, 69, 70; the ideal other 66, 70 *see also* idealisation/the ideal; intrusion into *see* intrusion; the presence of 71–2, 110; self-objectifying through 74; self–other interplay 26, 46; voyeurism and *see* voyeurism
overdetermination 45, 71, 81, 100
overload 95, 101, 106

parental breakup 41–2
'passage' as a signifier 50–1
past, and history 30–1
paternal matters *see* fathers/the paternal
perception: period of hesitation 150, 151; unconscious 16, 17, 70, 126, 151
persistence 35–6, 43–5, 130, 133; in questioning 136
phonemes: chains of meaning 50–1, 73; clusters 26–7; signifiers xi, 26–7, 50–1, 73; *see also* sonic category of unconscious expression
Plato 152
play: between self and other 26, 46; playing on others' weaknesses 92–3, 103–4
potential space 108, 121, 151
preconceptual knowledge 130
the preconscious xiii–xiv
problem solving: hope that the problem will solve itself 35, 36, 43, 44; through persistence 43–4; saying something only once 35–6, 38, 43, 44, 47, 51–2

projection: circuitive 88; defence and 114–15; projective identification 37, 41, 79, 87–8; projective narration 90; projective thinking 57, 69–70, 87–8; proxies 57, 109; transference and 88, 90; of the true self 66
proxies 57, 109
psychic intensities 1
psycho-development 44; *see also* self-development
psychoanalysis: analytical sessions *see* analytical sessions; British/French differences 115; creativity of 16–17; dream work *see* dream work; and the encounter of the oddity 149; the 'Freudian Pair' 19–22, 119–21, 137–8; the ignoring of the unrepressed unconscious xi, 2, 16, 17; interpretation *see* interpretation; as a repressive force 16; supervision 21, 32; and unconscious insight about the 'need for two' 67, 71; work situated in unconscious intersubjectivity 14; as a working partnership 19–22, 119–21; *see also* unconscious work
psychoanalysts *see* analysts
psychoanalytic process *see* analytical process
psychosis 97

questioning: answered by the questioner's unconscious 52, 54, 57, 72, 106–7, 109; and dream formation 127–8; as the drive behind the thought process 22–3; echoing 123; and the enigmatic signifier 147; the epistemophilic drive 141, 142, 144–5, 146, 153; explicit questions 22, 54; in *Hamlet* (Shakespeare) 142–4, 149; and human freedom 23; humanity of 147–8; implicit questions 16, 22; interrogative drive of the associative 150; interrogative imperative 72; interrogative position 148;